High-Impact Presentation and Training Skills —
Proven Techniques for Captivating, Motivating and Inspiring

By

Dr. William Hendricks
Micki Holliday
Recie Mobley
Kristy Steinbrecher

National Press Publications

A Division of Rockhurst College Continuing Education Center, Inc.
6901 West 63rd Street • Shawnee Mission, KS 66201-1349
1-800-258-7248 • 1-913-432-7757

High-Impact Presentation and Training Skills — Proven Techniques for Captivating, Motivating and Inspiring
Published by National Press Publications, Inc.
A Division of Rockhurst College Continuing Education Center, Inc.

©1994, Rockhurst College Continuing Education Center, Inc.

Printed in the United States of America

5 6 7 8 9

ISBN # 1-55852-131-3

About Rockhurst College Continuing Education Center, Inc.

Rockhurst College Continuing Education Center, Inc., is committed to providing lifelong learning opportunities through the integration of innovative education and training.

National Seminars Group, a division of Rockhurst College Continuing Education Center, Inc., has its finger on the pulse of America's business community. We've trained more than 2 million people in every imaginable occupation to be more productive and advance their careers. Along the way, we've learned a few things. Like what it takes to be successful ... how to build the skills to make it happen ... and how to translate learning into results. Millions of people from thousands of companies around the world turn to National Seminars for training solutions.

National Press Publications is our product and publishing division. We offer a complete line of the finest self-study and continuing-learning resources available anywhere. These products present our industry-acclaimed curriculum and training expertise in a concise, action-oriented format you can put to work right away. Packed with real-world strategies and hands-on techniques, these resources are guaranteed to help you meet the career and personal challenges you face every day.

Legend Symbol Guide

Exercises that reinforce your learning experience.

Questions that will help you apply the critical points to your situation.

Checklist that will help you identify important issues for future application.

Key issues to learn and understand for future application.

C A S E S T U D Y

Real-world case studies that will help you apply the information you've learned.

Introduction

If you had a product that worked well, was recognized as the industry standard for quality and consistency and people kept asking you to teach them what you know, what would you do? We wrote a book! We took what we are known for — *high-quality, high-impact* presentations — and broke it into understandable pieces.

"Talk is cheap," according to the old saying, but surveys show most Americans would rather do just about *anything* than get up in front of a group and speak. In fact, most people rate the fear of public speaking higher than they rate the fear of death! Are you one of those folks who has always claimed you'd rather die than make a presentation before your company? Then this book was written for you. Consider it not only a lifesaver, but a career enhancer.

High-Impact Presentation and Training Skills — Proven Techniques for Captivating, Motivating and Inspiring is divided into three sections. In chapters 1-5, you'll discover the key to controlling your fears, as well as how to outline and organize an effective presentation. Chapters 6-9 focus on delivery and the importance of capturing and maintaining the attention of your audience. Chapters 10-14 deal with developing your skills as a trainer. After all, training is nothing but a presentation on how to do something!

Our goal is simple. We want you to succeed in your career and to learn the tricks of the trade that every professional speaker uses to get focused and energized.

In addition, you'll learn:
- tips to ensure a smooth presentation
- how to size up any audience
- techniques to build rapport
- how to identify your personal presentation style
- tips for using audio/visual materials
- how to deal with hostile people
- the importance of listening well
- how people learn
- when training would and would not be beneficial

The time you spend learning the techniques of a skillful presenter and trainer is time you're investing in your future success. When you make powerful presentations, you'll make yourself invaluable to your company.

About the Authors ...

National Seminars Group is responsible for making more than 6,000 business presentations a year. The audiences range from 15 executives in a boardroom to 250 front-line customer service representatives. Each presentation comes with this consistent demand: "be engaging, be factual and present your material in a way that it can be used." Since 1984 National Seminars Group has grown to become the nation's largest university-based business training center in the world. Hundreds of today's top speakers have been trained in a proven methodology for gaining and maintaining an audience's attention, whether that's an audience of one or a thousand and one in number. Four of the people responsible for this success turned their daily jobs — making successful presentations — into this book. Here's who they are, and a portion of what each brings to the discipline of developing training and presentation skills.

Recie Mobley, Director of Faculty, is responsible for placing competently trained professionals in front of more than 500,000 people a year. Her skill at bringing out one's natural talents is unmatched. She knows how to build and affirm speakers' strengths, so their true passion is delivered in every talk or training session they give. In the pages that follow, you'll notice the positive and affirming tone Recie brings to her profession. She knows how to make every presenter believe "it's OK to be me."

Micki Holliday, Manager of Training at National Seminars, is unmatched in building the bridges between "what must be said" and "what can be heard" by the audience. Micki works day in and day out in front of audiences. As a professional speaker, Micki addresses thousands of people annually. As a trainer of professional speakers, she impacts hundreds of America's largest corporations. Micki illuminates this book. You'll feel her personality throughout the pages.

Kristy Steinbrecher, Curriculum Specialist at National Seminars, customizes curriculum for the specialized needs of more than 50 corporations per month. She keeps everyone focused on the real-world realities. Her direct, deliberate, to-the-point methodology provides practical advice on nearly every page.

Dr. William Hendricks is Director of Curriculum at National Seminars. I get the privilege of acting as the editor for this tremendous team of presentation specialists. My responsibility is for the annual development of more than 140 training products in the form of books, tapes and seminars. I'm dedicated to consistent, accurate and contemporary materials which I hope you find reflected in the substance of this book.

Preface

How many times have you sat and listened to a dynamic presenter and thought enviously, "Wow, some people are just born speakers! I'd faint flat on the floor if I had to get up in front of a crowd"?

Truth is, effective speakers aren't "born." They are developed over time, and they continue to hone their skills, learning from each and every presentation they make. It has been my experience that even the most polished speakers suffer a few "butterflies" now and again, but these seasoned presenters have learned how to channel that nervous energy into delivering a message that packs a real punch.

Ask yourself honestly: What would it mean to you, both personally and professionally, if you could deliver a top-notch presentation to a group or conduct a first-rate training session for your company? I'll tell you what it could mean: It could mean an increase in self-confidence you never thought possible. It could mean you'll be labeled an "up-and-comer" in your organization. It could mean unlimited career potential.

This book is in your hands because you've made a commitment to yourself and to your future. The presentation skills you have the opportunity to acquire from these chapters will open doors for you for the rest of your life.

So read on: Don't be left out in the cold!

Dr. Bill Hendricks
Director of Curriculum
National Seminars Group

Table of Contents

C HAPTER 1

Getting Started

You have just learned that your boss wants you to make a presentation on the company's manufacturing capabilities a week from Tuesday. What is your first response? If you are like most people, it's fear.

In *The Book of Lists,* New York, William Morrow & Co., Inc., 1977, by David Wallechinsky, Irving Wallace, and Amy Wallace, the authors surveyed participants to name their 14 worst fears. Forty-one percent said number one was speaking before a group.

Although public speaking is the number one fear of most people, you don't have to panic. All speakers, even professional ones, experience some amount of fear before giving a presentation. The secret is to take that fear and make it work for you instead of against you. Fear produces nervous energy. By confronting the fear, you can convert your nervous energy into presentational energy.

Here are some ways to channel nervousness:

1. Walk around the room of the presentation prior to the arrival of the audience, making it your own.
2. Meet and greet the audience, shaking hands and building friendship bridges.
3. Go to an out-of-sight area and bend from the waist, letting hands and arms drop to the ground.
4. Take deep breaths, letting the air out slowly.
5. Tense and relax muscles in your face, arms, stomach and legs.
6. Stretch your neck, arms and legs.

> *"Do the thing you fear, and the death of fear is certain."*
> Ralph Waldo Emerson

1

7. Concentrate on your success.
8. Visualize the audience as you want them to act immediately after the presentation.
9. Engage in self-talk about your excellent presentation.

Why do people fear public speaking? Here are just a few of the most common reasons given.

> *"In the last resort, nothing is ridiculous except the fear of being so."*
> Henri Fauconnier

1. Saying or doing something to embarrass themselves.

2. Saying or doing something that will ultimately damage their career or reputation.

3. Fear of making a fool of themselves.

4. Fear of forgetting what they are going to say.

5. Fear that others will see them as lacking.

6. Fear of rejection.

7. Fear that no one will respond.

8. Fear that someone will question them and they won't know the answer.

Understanding Fear

If you have a fear of standing before people and speaking, the first thing you need to do is ask yourself why. For most people, fear comes as a result of self-made expectations or worry. Research shows that 75 percent of the things that we worry about, or fear, never happen. Let's examine a few typical fears.

• **Fear #1:**

> What happens if I start my presentation and I forget everything I was going to say?

• **Reality:**

> If you have prepared and practiced your presentation, this is highly unlikely. Besides, you will have notes to refresh your memory in the event you do forget.

• **Two Tips:**

> 1. Regardless of your preparedness, have sufficient notes within easy reach. In the event you draw a blank, you can refer to them for an idea. No matter how well you are prepared or how well you know the subject, always have written support available to fall back on.
>
> 2. Have two or three "Buy-Time" questions prepared. If you do forget what to say or where your presentation is going, you can "Buy some time."

> *"Courage is resistance to fear, mastery of fear — not absence of fear."*
> Mark Twain

"Buy-Time" questions do just that — they buy you time with the audience so you can collect your thoughts. They are questions that are broad enough to take some time for the listeners to answer, and yet the answers are not necessary to review for your presentation flow. They simply keep the audience occupied for a moment or two while you get back into your presentation.

For example: As you are presenting a report on recent changes in employment law, you draw a blank. You have no idea what point you were trying to make or where you were going with it. You pause and say: "Let's stop and consider the impact of these issues on your particular departments. Please take a few moments to identify three instances where this has an impact on your overall work flow."

Some additional examples of "Buy-Time" questions include:

- Take a moment and identify three instances on the job where these points apply.
- Note three strengths you have that would support the points just stated, and three areas of concern given your style of management.

- Think of a time when you encountered these concerns. How would you handle them now, given this information?
- Identify an associate who has these responsibilities and consider how this knowledge could benefit his overall job effectiveness.
- Consider the challenges that the business faces because of the current climate in the industry, and prioritize your top three issues.

The key to "Buy-Time" questions is that they are specific enough to have relevance to your theme, and general enough to take some thought on the part of the audience.

Fear #2:

What happens if I do something to embarrass myself?

Reality:

Unless it is a major faux pas, chances are you will be the only person aware of it. And, in the event you do something clearly noticeable, like trip up the stairs, try using the experience to interject some humor into your presentation or, if possible, relate it to your presentation, making it seem planned. For example, "When I just tripped up the stairs, I could have really hurt myself. If I had, it's nice to know that our company has a health insurance plan that would take care of all of my doctor bills. The company's health insurance plan is what I would like to talk to you about today."

This example illustrates the importance of maintaining your control of the situation and yourself. Regardless of what occurs, turn it to your benefit. If you can immediately identify an adverse situation and handle it, you neutralize it. In effect, you pull it out of the audience's thoughts.

> *"When you have a lemon, make lemonade."*
> Julius Rosenwald

4

Fear #3:

What happens if I make a fool of myself?

Reality:

This is a fairly common fear. But ask yourself, what could you possibly do that would make you look foolish? You probably won't be able to think of anything that's within reason. If you do, plan for it.

If, during your preparation time, you consider worst-case scenarios and you have a plan for each, you can minimize the possibility of "beyond" reasonable fears. For example, "WHAT IF"...

> *"Remember, fear doesn't exist anywhere except in the mind."*
> Dale Carnegie

1. What if I slur my words?
2. What if I say the wrong thing?
3. What if an unmentionable noise comes out of my mouth?

Regardless of the WHAT-IFS, you know you have options. You can:
1. Ignore the gaffe, look the audience straight in the eyes and move on.
2. Pause, note the gaffe (e.g., "that's a tough one") and move on.
3. Call a break and take time in private to gain control.
4. Use a "Buy-Time" question to regroup.

You can do all sorts of things ... IF you prepare. The trick is to maintain control. And, you do this by knowing you have choices.

Fear #4:

What happens if I say or do something that damages my career or reputation?

Reality:

This is a pretty unrealistic fear, especially if you are prepared. Keep things in perspective. This is a single presentation. It's very unlikely that your entire career or reputation will depend on one presentation. If you can't bring yourself to make presentations, however, it could hurt your chances for future promotions.

Consider your options, both short and long-term. What are the immediate gains of doing this presentation? Are they greater than the potential losses? Will you have another chance? What are the expectations of your boss, your customers, your associates? Often, timing has a lot to do with winning.

If the rewards are real, they can motivate you to make a plan and present an excellent report. For example, after deciding the gains are worth it, you could plan on "small is beautiful," and have a briefer-than-usual presentation, yet one that serves the purpose, thus lessening your agony.

Success is the best instructor. Set yourself up for the win and build on that. Next time, you can add more of the detail.

"Courage ... is the quality which guarantees all others."
Winston Churchill

Overcoming Fear

Once you understand your fears, you can begin to overcome them. To review, the three steps for overcoming your fears are:

Step 1. Identify the fear. Be specific. For example, "I am afraid I won't make a good presentation and the boss will reject my budget." "I may get fired." "They may laugh at me." "I may forget."

Step 2. Identify the worst-case scenario. Plan for any and every situation before, during and after a presentation. Preparation and planning are the professional speaker's keys to overcoming fears.

Step 3. Next, ask yourself, "So what?" Using the previous example, "So what if my boss rejects my budget? I will find out what he finds unsatisfactory, redo the budget and present it again."

Exercise

Make a list of your fears about making presentations. Next to each, write down one or two words that describe the "worst case." Next, write down the possible impact of your fear.

Fear	Worst Case Scenario	"So What?"
_____	_____	_____
_____	_____	_____
_____	_____	_____
_____	_____	_____
_____	_____	_____
_____	_____	_____
_____	_____	_____
_____	_____	_____
_____	_____	_____
_____	_____	_____
_____	_____	_____
_____	_____	_____

Using Self-Talk

The number one factor that determines individual success or failure is SELF-ESTEEM — how you feel about you. All of us talk to ourselves, approximately 70 percent of the time in any given day. This is known to you through your self-talk. And if that isn't surprising, note that while the average person may speak aloud at a rate of 150 to 250 words per minute, the average self-talk occurs at rates in excess of 800 wpm! The issue is not **whether** it is occurring — the issue is **what** you are saying. The sad fact is that most of us have "little gremlins" — all those shoulda, woulda, couldas, and even more harmful "nasties" — that chip away at our self-esteem, feeding on our fears, sending inaccurate messages that blur fear and reality. Studies confirm that the average person has a multitude of these negative messages circulating in his mind at any given moment.

Yet you can turn these messages from negative barriers to positive affirmations. Whatever you put into your mind, in one way or another, is what you get out. You can program yourself with supportive messages through conscious, positive self-talk. It may be awkward at first; however, it is the easiest and fastest way to new behaviors, like improved presentation skills. You can curse, nurse, rehearse or REVERSE the negative self-talk that perpetuates failure.

Positive self-talk reverses fears by overriding them. It instills confidence, and confidence allows action — actions you can take to overcome any fear.

Self-talk is exactly what it sounds like — talking to yourself about a problem. Negative self-talk magnifies fears, promotes self-doubt and instills "I can't" thinking. Positive self-talk focuses on possibilities, positive outcomes and "can do" thinking. Effective self-talk can help you put things in perspective.

> *"Our life is what our thoughts make it."*
> Marcus Aurelius

Listed below are examples of negative self-talk. Notice how the exaggerated, unrealistic outcomes instill "I can't" thinking.

"I don't want to make this presentation. I'm afraid I am going to make a fool of myself."

"I'll never forget when I was in high school and the teacher picked me to read a poem. I fumbled through most of it and the other students laughed."

Read the following examples of positive self-talk. Notice how rational thought has replaced irrational fear.

"Yes, but this isn't high school. Unlike then, I now have the opportunity to prepare and practice for my presentation. And, unlike high school, I will be addressing adults, not teen-agers. Adults are more tolerant."

"Besides, my boss wouldn't have asked me to make this presentation if he didn't have confidence in me. I know that if I prepare well and practice, I can do it!"

> *"A man is what he thinks about all day long."*
> Ralph Waldo Emerson

How to Overcome Your Fear of Public Speaking

You can use self-talk to help you overcome your fear of presentations. To do so, follow the guide below.

1. Tell yourself what you are afraid of. Example: Speaking before a group.

2. Explain to yourself why you have this fear. Example: I have always felt I would die if I had to stand up and talk before people.

3. Rationalize why this shouldn't be a fear. Example: I've never spoken in front of a group, so why do I think this? I don't know anyone who has spoken before a group who died from it.

4. Close with a positive statement about yourself and your ability to make the presentation. Example: I am a clever and knowledgeable person. I learn fast. I can do whatever I plan to do.

There IS magic to help overcome the fear of making presentations. It is the affirmations you tell yourself — the positive self-talk that you consciously program to REVERSE the fears and negative barriers. It may help to realize that there are a lot of others who share these fears and limitations, and a lot who have succeeded in "taming the gremlins."

The uneasy feelings many share are "butterflies." To paraphrase a famous quote, the issue is not the butterflies, but getting them to fly in formation.

To be the best possible presenter, don't ever lose those butterflies — not completely. Use them to boost your positive self-talk. Control your butterflies. Don't let them control you. Use the extra adrenaline produced by your nerves to help charge you up. They help keep you on your toes. If you don't get somewhat nervous, it means that making presentations has become routine for you, and your presentations will reflect that attitude.

Four Facts About Fear

If you let it, fear will immobilize you. The trick is to overcome fear, so that instead of immobilizing you, it energizes you. When thinking about fear, consider the following statements.

1. Fear will never go away as long as you continue to grow. There is a certain amount of fear involved in growing. Change is inevitable. If you have nothing to be afraid of, you've become stagnant. Nothing in life stays the same; all things in nature are either growing or they are regressing.

2. The only way to ease the fear of doing something is to go out and do it. If you are afraid of speaking in front of groups, take every opportunity you get to do just that. Public speaking gets easier and easier every time you do it. Some opportunities might include the PTA or PTO in your area school, a church organization, political events or heading an informal discussion at a business meeting.

3. You're not the only one to experience fear when you're in unfamiliar territory. Anyone who has ever spoken in front of a group has experienced fear just like you. Because of that, you can be assured that the group you are addressing will be empathetic and understanding if you appear a little nervous. Many people bolster their self-esteem by realizing that they are not alone out there, that others have and are experiencing similar things.

4. Living through a fearful experience is less frightening than living with the underlying fear that comes from helplessness. Although you may be afraid to stand in front of a crowd and speak, doing so will last only a few minutes or hours. If you never conquer your fear of public speaking, that fear will hang over your head forever. You have choices.

> *"Self-confidence is the first requisite to great undertakings."*
> Samuel Johnson

Neil Armstrong, the first astronaut to walk on the moon, was asked if he was ever afraid. He replied, "There I was, atop the Saturn 500, over 10,000 bits and pieces, all made by the lowest bidder. Sometimes there is good reason."

Projecting the Best Possible Image

Once you've started to overcome your fear, you will want to project the best possible image. Advertising research has shown that people form an opinion of you within the first five to seven seconds after they see you standing before them. In making any presentation, it is important for you to project a positive image — even before you begin to speak. Your self-image derives from your self-esteem and in turn boosts your self-esteem. They work hand-in-hand.

In order to project a positive image, you need to work on those factors over which you have control: your dress, mood, tone and expertise.

- **DRESS.** Dress can provide you with increased confidence that will be reflected in everything you do and say. Make sure your dress communicates a professional image. Your clothes should be neatly pressed and your shoes polished.

Some tips:

- Dress conservatively — unless you are in an industry that thrives on individuality.
- Identify the acceptable form of attire for the group you are addressing and dress one step above your audience.
- Women are usually more effective wearing a suit or a skirt and jacket.
- Power colors include any blue, any gray and most jewel tones.
- Pearls add credibility, while anything dangling distracts from the speaker's presentation.
- Men are generally dressed appropriately in a suit.

Additionally, your hair should be neatly styled and your fingernails neatly trimmed. Consider going to a stylist or beautician a few days prior to the presentation. Paying attention to these details will help convey a business-like image that will get your presentation off to a good start. And, it can add to your self-confidence.

- **MOOD.** Temperament influences everything you do. Research has shown time and again how it also affects those around you. Consider the results of engaging in a job interview immediately after being fired and before you have resolved all those negative and ambivalent feelings about the previous situation and employer. How will you appear to the interviewer, regardless of how controlled and careful you are?

Imagine a salesperson who is attempting to convince a customer to purchase a product that the salesperson dislikes immensely and has tried repeatedly to remove from the product line. How is this salesperson going to sell the product's benefits?

Or, can a jury be expected to make its decision based solely on the evidence documented during the trial, or is the manner in which the attorneys frowned, hesitated and appeared to react to specific testimony going to weigh heavily on the jury's deliberations?

> *Power colors include any blue or gray and most jewel tones.*

It is important that you appear upbeat when making a presentation. If you come across as uncaring or distracted, you're going to have a hard time selling your idea. Check your feelings and emotions at the door and deal with them after your presentation.

What can you do about mood? Plenty, once you realize how it can help or hinder your presentation.

1. The term "shake it off" is most relevant here. Shake it off by concentrating on your content.
2. Discipline yourself to "think about it tomorrow" as Scarlett O'Hara did. Perhaps write it down in your calendar to attend to later, at a specific time. Then, close the book.
3. Take deep breaths.
4. "Fake it 'til you make it." The more unhappy your mood, the more you must smile, move into the audience, act relaxed and project an air that you are enjoying yourself. And what's amazing, you will!

- **TONE.** When making your presentation, use a confident, well-controlled tone of voice. If your tone lacks confidence, people won't give your ideas much credence, and if your voice is too gruff, people will turn you off. Practice is essential here.

1. Tape yourself. Listen for rate, volume and emphasis. Are you easy to listen to? Practice raising and lowering your voice. Planning when to raise or lower your voice can be cued by a special color in your notes.
2. Inflection can be planned. Note your words and intention and plan how to make one word stand out in a sentence. Example: "HE is an excellent resource" vs. "he is an excellent RESOURCE." Depending upon the emphasis, the meaning can be changed.

> *"I like a man who bubbles over with enthusiasm. Better be a geyser than a mud puddle."*
> John G. Shedd

1

3. Slow down for important points. Research indicates that a fast rate of speech can have positive and negative impact. People prefer speakers with a fast rate of speech (above the norm of 125 to 250 wpm); but if it is too fast, audiences become frustrated. So, speed up periodically to carry your audience along.
4. Note that a high voice as well as speaking too rapidly indicates nervousness; thus the reverse, a slower, lower tone, conveys confidence.

"We are not who we are but what is said of us and what we read in others' eyes."
Mary, Queen of Scots

*   **EXPERTISE.** Before making any presentation, make sure you are thoroughly familiar with the topic. For example, if you are asked to give a presentation to your team about your company's new product, make sure that you do your homework.

Some tips to increase your expertise:

1. Review annual reports.
2. Talk to customers (users).
3. Ask people who are more experienced and knowledgeable.
4. Read books and articles on the subject.

Image Checklist

Before making your next presentation, use the following checklist to help you project your best possible image:

☐ I identified typical attire for my audience.

☐ I chose what to wear based on audience preference and expectation.

☐ My clothes are appropriate.
- 10 percent above audience's level of dress
- neatly pressed
- accessories correct – they enhance, not detract

☐ My shoes have been polished and are not worn out.

☐ My fingernails have been manicured or neatly trimmed.

☐ My hair is stylish, acceptable to the audience and neatly combed.

☐ I feel comfortable and confident in these clothes.

☐ My mood is upbeat.

☐ I have done my research and I am thoroughly familiar with the topic.

☐ I have practiced my presentation, concentrating on the tone of my voice.

To Speak or Not to Speak

Sometimes you will be able to choose to make a presentation, other times you won't. If you have a choice, accept only those speaking engagements that you can do without conducting any research. That doesn't mean that you won't do research — it simply means you won't have to do an extensive amount in order to feel confident.

For example, you are asked to make a presentation to your company's board of directors, concerning the new customer satisfaction policies developed and implemented by your department. You have been involved in all the meetings, have an abundance of notes, are familiar with the references and sources used in making decisions, and can cite examples of successful and unsuccessful companies. In short, while you are not prepared to speak at this moment, you have the knowledge and awareness to deliver an impressive presentation with minimal preparation.

Before accepting a speaking assignment, ask yourself the following questions.

> *"I shall never be old enough to speak without embarrassment when I have nothing to say."*
> Abraham Lincoln

1. Have I earned the right to talk about this subject? Example: I've worked with this subject for years; or: I've been in this industry for some time; or: this is something in which I believe strongly.

2. Am I excited about this subject? Do I care? How has it affected me? Why? How does it relate to my experience?

3. Am I eager to share this information with another person? What are my beliefs on this subject, about its relevance and usefulness?

If you can respond positively to the above questions, this is a speaking engagement you should accept. If your responses are negative, gracefully decline and be prepared to suggest someone else who might be more qualified.

Confidence in yourself is essential.

How to Avoid Self-Destruction

As you begin making presentations to others, there are some pitfalls that every professional presenter learns to overcome. Check this list carefully, because many speakers destruct in front of their audience — not because they are poorly prepared, but because they make fundamental mistakes that are easy to avoid. Five common sources of self-destruction are given below.

> *Don't borrow undue authority. Be an authority.*

1. **Expert overload.** Many speakers cite so many experts and quote so many resources, they compete with their own expertise. The audience members begin to ask themselves, "Does this person know anything on his own?" Don't forget that they considered *your* knowledge valuable. You should know the experts and you should have the justification from research in your mind, but the presentation should be yours. Don't borrow undue authority. Be an authority.

2. **Speaking vs. communicating.** As an expert, especially when discussing technical subjects, it is easy to speak and not communicate. Effective speaking builds dialogue, not monologue. The great public speakers make the audience members feel that they are having a conversation with the speaker, even when the room is packed with hundreds of people. Thinking and responding for the audience, addressing the audience's needs and making sure that audience's agenda is being addressed are some of the most overlooked and easily corrected pitfalls of public speaking.

3. **Lack of audience control.** Many speakers get trapped when fielding questions from an audience. Here's how it occurs. A simple and direct question is asked by a member of the audience, but before the speaker can answer the question, someone in the room responds, often adding some new information. And the "chain-reaction" begins. A speaker can lose control very quickly, especially if the "add-on" information is incorrect or volatile in nature. Remember, the speaker is responsible for the agenda and

1

the emotions of that room. To regain control, stop the chain-reaction, return to the original question, answer it and then set aside the other issues for a future meeting when facts and people can be prepared to discuss it.

4. **Credibility issues.** Two common techniques used by audiences to test the knowledge of the speaker are "Stump-the-Chump" and "Ask Mr. Fix-It." Both are deadly to a speaker's credibility and both pull on the same emotional cords, your ego. When a speaker is perceived as knowledgeable, the "Mr./Ms. Fix-It" technique occurs. The audience believes that the speaker can "fix" or answer any concern or question. The danger here is that, in an attempt to maintain this belief, the speaker offers answers that are not founded. There is no crime in saying, "I don't know." But there *is* a fatal flaw in many people who feel they must be able to respond and know everything. When a speaker is perceived as unknowing, "Stump-the-Chump" is a common audience ploy. Bizarre, irrelevant questions are asked in rapid succession, in an attempt to "de-throne" or humiliate. The danger in this technique is simple ... they could be right! If you are widely perceived as unknowledgeable, you probably are.

5. **Information overload.** Another pitfall speakers frequently stumble over is information overload. Because you are an expert in the areas being discussed, because you have more information than the majority of the audience and because you frequently have a greater sense of "imparting knowledge," it's easy to cram too much information into the presentation. Attention spans fragment and people hear only bits and pieces of what they need to know. The "KISS — Keep It Simple, Stupid" — formula should always be remembered.

"I was gratified to answer promptly, and I did. I said I didn't know."
Mark Twain

Questions for Personal Development

1. What is the major emphasis of Getting Started?

    _____

    _____

    _____

2. What are the most important things you learned from this chapter?

    _____

    _____

    _____

3. How can you apply what you learned to your current job?

    _____

    _____

    _____

4. How will you go about making these improvements?

    _____

    _____

    _____

5. How can you monitor your improvement?

_____

_____

_____

6. Summarize the changes you expect to see in yourself one year from now.

_____

_____

_____

Summary

If you get nervous at the thought of making a presentation, don't worry, you aren't alone. Most people, even professional speakers, experience a certain amount of nervousness. The key is to control your fear instead of letting it control you.

In order to control your fear, you must first identify exactly what it is that you are afraid of. Once you've identified your fear, you can use positive self-talk and rationalization to help overcome it.

The best way to overcome a fear is to tackle it head-on. Therefore, if presentations make you nervous, do them every chance you get. With each one you make, you will become more comfortable and self-confident.

Improve those things over which you have control, such as your preparation, practice, dress, mood, tone and expertise. Doing so will help make you feel more confident and help you project a positive, professional image that will get your presentation off to a good start.

If you have a choice about making a presentation, choose only those topics you will feel comfortable discussing. If you don't feel comfortable giving a presentation, politely decline and suggest someone more qualified.

In Chapter 1 you began to prepare yourself as a presenter. In Chapter 2 you will learn about your audience.

*C*HAPTER 2

Knowing Your Audience

Knowing something about the audience will help you not only in preparing for your presentation, but also in making your presentation. In this chapter, you will learn how to address various groups of people, as well as to identify individual personality types. Knowing this information will help you target a successful presentation to a specific audience.

Size of the Group

The size of the group you're speaking to will affect your content, logistics and presentation style. When addressing fewer than 30 people you have more flexibility. Your presentation can be relatively informal, you have more chances for one-on-one rapport and you can make eye contact with everyone in the room.

Although 30 to 50 people is still considered a small group, you have less flexibility. You should be able to make eye contact with just about everyone in the room. If there is a need for group discussion, you can ask participants to break into small groups of five or 10.

Addressing more than 50 people creates some challenges. With a group this large, it is difficult to make eye contact with everyone, and you may need a microphone in order to be heard. If so, try to get a lapel microphone so that you can move around.

> *Know your stuff, know whom you are stuffing, and know when they are stuffed.*

The following chart illustrates how audience size affects your presentation. Notice the shift in emphasis as group size increases.

Presentation Skills Continuum

**Big Room
Presentation Skills**
• Speaker centered
• Limited overheads
• Simple visuals

**Structured
Group Dynamic Skills**
• Content/Speaker centered
• Targeted overheads
• Application visuals

**Interactive
Training Skills**
• Content centered
• Unlimited overheads
• Content-specific visuals

**Small Group
Facilitation Skills**
• Audience centered
• Hand-written overheads
• Customer-relevant visuals

Speaker Dominance

Audience Size

Audience size affects your presentation style.

Audience size affects how you will present a topic and how you will target it to a specific audience. Getting an audience on your side requires topic relevancy, content and example specificity, and speaker expertise.

Audience size affects your presentation style; whether you are formal or informal, direct or indirect, if you need scheduled or impromptu breaks, whether you can have high interaction or limited interaction, and what tools you will be able to use. How you handle the audience members and make them your partner requires different techniques for different sizes of groups.

For example:
- With groups of 3 to 6 people, you can be very conversant in your approach, relaxed and for the most part able to let the individuals dictate pace and formality. Names are a requirement.
- With groups of 10 to 12, more scheduled activities are required. You will need to consider how to arrange the room, when to have breaks and what type of support materials you need. Group activities are conducive to learning.
- Groups of 20 require more planning. Larger size groups eliminate the ability to use certain audio/visuals, as visibility becomes an important factor. A more formal approach with more control is required.

When addressing your superiors, suggest — don't lecture or dictate.

Makeup of the Audience

How you address your audience will depend greatly on whom you are addressing. Are you making a presentation to the board of directors about the company's new marketing plan, or are you telling your team how to deal with stress? Consider the following tips when addressing various groups of people.

- *Superiors*: When addressing your superiors, suggest — don't lecture or dictate. Back everything you say with facts. Plan to be slightly formal in your presentation. Example: "These are some of my suggestions for you to consider when deciding the best direction in which to go. Number one is ..."

- *Peers:* When talking with your peers, relate or share information. But be careful not to engage in one-upmanship. Draw them into the presentation and ask them to share their expertise and experiences. You may have luck if you admit some errors and are slightly vulnerable.

2

- *Team Members*: When addressing members of your team, relate facts or details through demonstration and the use of examples. Make sure you use "we" language. A good guideline when talking to team members is to share success and accept the blame.

- *Special Interest Groups:* In addressing special interest groups, be sure to focus your presentation around the concerns of that particular group. Relate by persuading, convincing or giving opinions. For example, if you work for a company that manufactures motor oil and you are talking to an environmental group, don't tell them why your oil is the best product on the market, tell them about your company's public campaign to safely dispose of motor oil.

- *Mixed Groups*: If the group you are addressing contains a mix of people — team members and peers — you will need to use a combination of presentation techniques in order to reach everyone. Make sure you capture each group within the first few minutes by using examples, jargon or making references to each one.

Expertise of the Audience

> *When they are interested,*
> *teach them.*
> *When they don't want to be there,*
> *involve them.*
> *When they are uninterested,*
> *entertain them.*

The expertise of the audience determines how you present your facts and what you say about the topic. A good standard to use is: When the group members are interested and want to be there, *teach* them through your presentation. When they are dubious or don't want to be there, *involve* them. When they are bored, uninterested or haven't any idea why they are there, *entertain* them.

What is the level of expertise of the people you are addressing? Are they informed? If so, they will be familiar with your topic, so suggest rather than tell them information. And be careful not to talk down to them. Perhaps your audience is uninformed. If that's the case, your best approach will be to instruct or teach.

Are you addressing a technical audience? For example, a group of engineers? If so, be logical and analytical when presenting your information.

Your Expectations

2

What are your expectations for your presentation? First, how much time have you been allotted? Second, how much time do you need? If someone else asks you to make the presentation, he will probably tell you how long you have. If you are scheduling the presentation, be sensitive to the audience's time constraints and availability. For example, if you ask your associates to meet after work, you probably should make your presentation as brief as possible so they can get home at a reasonable hour. Expectations determine your overall timing and structure, so tailor the presentation around audience expectations, as well as your own.

With regard to preparation and development, a good guideline is four hours of preparation are generally required for every hour of presentation. That is, IF you have all knowledge and support materials available. For new materials, prep time is generally 8:1, eight hours of preparation for one hour of presentation.

In structuring times, consider the best and the worst times for yourself as well as for the audience. Are you a morning person or is your energy and concentration at its best in the afternoon? Audiences generally dislike Monday mornings and Friday afternoons. Tuesday mornings are often an optimal time for conducting presentations. An optimal time to ensure concentration is 10 a.m. Poor times for concentration occur around 11 - 11:30 a.m., 1 - 1:30 p.m. and 4 - 4:30 p.m.

Many audiences expect information to be presented in a standard format and style. It is what they are used to. For example, boards of directors expect, and are most comfortable with, formal presentations, whereas community affairs panels are often more casual in style and structure.

Will your presentation take the form of a discussion, a lecture or a combination of the two? Once again, this will depend on the size of the group. If you address fewer than 50 people, discussion is possible. Whether you include discussion also depends on what you hope to achieve. If your goal is to encourage sharing among peers, discussion is the best methodology.

Is the group receptive or hostile? If you are discussing company layoffs, chances are the group will be hostile. If you are explaining an upgrade in the company's benefit package, chances are the audience will be receptive.

Allow four hours of prep time for every hour of presentation.

2

The more you know about your audience and its attitude toward the subject matter prior to the presentation, the better prepared you can be. What are the "hot" topics, what are issues of import, what are the associates talking about? Are there any situations that have occurred, or are there any undercurrents? Audience feedback and interaction are critical components of any presentation's success.

> *Audience feedback is a critical component of a presentation's success.*

2

Copy the following worksheet and complete it before each presentation that you make. It will help you analyze the audience so that you can tailor your presentation accordingly.

Audience Analysis Worksheet

1. Size:
   - ☐ 1-10
   - ☐ 11-20
   - ☐ 21-30
   - ☐ 31-50
   - ☐ 51+

2. Makeup:
   - ☐ Superiors
   - ☐ Peers
   - ☐ Your work team
   - ☐ Special interest groups
     (identify special interest: _____)
   - ☐ Mixed group

3. Expertise:
   - ☐ Informed
   - ☐ Uninformed
   - ☐ Technical
   - ☐ General

4. Expectations:
   - ☐ Time: _____
   - ☐ Formal   ☐ Informal
   - ☐ Discussion   ☐ Lecture   ☐ Combination
   - ☐ Receptive   ☐ Hostile

Individual Personalities

Once you know the overall makeup of your audience, it's important for you to consider individual personalities. By going from an audience to an individual analysis, you leave nothing to chance. You are ready to capitalize on every possible opportunity.

You must maintain your focus on the audience as a whole and not any one individual. The fact is that audiences do have "herd mentalities," and they often react collectively to presentations, based upon the reactions of key individuals.

Knowing something about the personalities of the people you will address helps you develop a customized presentation. This information also will help you to "play" to your audience. Saying the right things in the right way will make audience members more likely to buy into what you are telling them.

Some components to consider include:

1. What motivates the group members in a learning environment; how committed are they?
2. How do the audience members complete their work (psychomotor vs. psychological)?
3. How do they work with each other and react to authority?
4. Is this the most efficient time for this group?
5. How do the physical surroundings affect them?

Understanding what types of individuals are present in your audience will allow you to integrate on motivational cues. You can predict an associate's buy-in to any idea or proposal by understanding the broad categories of motivators.

The following diagram describes the four typical personality types and the basis for motivation.

> *Saying the right things in the right way makes audience members more likely to buy into what you are telling them.*

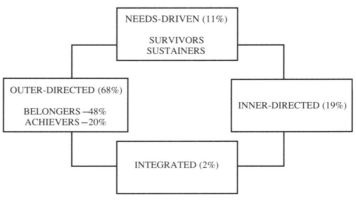

NEEDS-DRIVEN (11%)
SURVIVORS
SUSTAINERS

OUTER-DIRECTED (68%)
BELONGERS –48%
ACHIEVERS –20%

INNER-DIRECTED (19%)

INTEGRATED (2%)

- **Needs-Driven.** Within any group of people, you will find that roughly 11 percent are need-driven, also known as sustainers or survivors. These individuals are driven by their basic instincts. They act and respond to presentations that enhance their security and well-being. These individuals constantly filter information by thinking, "What's in it for me?"

How to identify needs-driven people: If you ask for a report on Friday, these individuals will give it to you on Friday — and not a moment sooner. They are not moved by inner forces or external events. It is the situation or the need of the moment that motivates them. It is the situation that pushes these individuals; they operate on a time-clock, knowing just how far they can push before they have to do something and what they get out of their actions.

How to reach needs-driven people: Give deadlines and explain the consequences if the deadline is not met. Be very specific about rewards and benefits in your presentations. For example, "I need to have all your reports on my desk tomorrow. If I don't, we won't be able to bid on the new project." In a presentation, be specific as to why something must be done. Keep materials relevant, concrete and oriented to personal interest when addressing this 11 percent of your audience.

- **Inner-Directed:** About one out of five, or 19 percent of people, is inner-directed. They move at their own paces. They have their own ways of getting things done. There is an internal motivator that causes these people to do the things they do. They dance to the beat of their own drummer. They have values that sustain them and are relevant to them. What others do does not inspire them.

How to identify inner-directed people: If you ask these individuals to complete a project, they will, but at their own pace. They don't like competition, so you probably won't find them moved by contests. Instead, they are more likely to bring their values and beliefs into your presentation, looking for points where they can have purpose.

> *About one out of five people is inner-directed.*

How to reach inner-directed people: Values are important to these people. Find out what is important to the inner-directed person and relate what you need in those terms. For example, an inner-directed individual may be a perfectionist who feels that everything must be done in just the right way. If that's the case, give that person assignments that require precision. To reach the inner-driven in a presentation, refer periodically to the specific values of this 19 percent. During your presentation, reiterate the overall goals of the organization, appealing to higher ideals. Create a big-picture context periodically. Show the humanness of your proposal or research, so they can align their values with your presentation.

> *Two-thirds of your audience will be outer-directed.*

- **Outer-Directed:** Two-thirds, or roughly 68 percent of your audience, will be outer-directed or externally driven. Of those, about 48 percent are belongers and 20 percent are achievers.

How to identify belongers. The belongers go along with the crowd. If they think everybody else is going to wear a suit, they wear a suit, too. They follow directions and fit in. They don't like to make waves. These are the individuals who respond to your presentation because other people like it. They enjoy being with others and talking about their families. Their feelings of success come from successful and happy relationships with their families and friends. You will probably find pictures of their families in their offices or work areas.

How to identify achievers. The achievers are your cheerleaders. They want to excel. The achievers are externally driven, and they strive towards well-defined standards of excellence. Rewards, excitement, competition, appraisals and feedback all stimulate these people. In their offices, achievers tend to have trophies, certificates or pictures of themselves winning something. They enjoy talking about goals and standards. They don't like playing the game if no one is keeping score. Sales groups tend to have a large number of achievers.

In a presentation where you do not know the audience, it is recommended that you structure your content to the 68 percent outer-directed group. However, throughout every group presentation, you must integrate thoughts and comments which appeal to each of the four motivator groups.

How to reach outer-directed people: Outer-directed people respond best to external rewards and regular feedback. In working with these individuals, establish contests or provide repeated recognition for accomplishments.

- **Integrated:** The remaining two percent of people are integrated. They are motivated in a variety of ways.

How to identify integrated people: Integrated people have a variety of the characteristics already mentioned. They enjoy being recognized publicly, yet they also are motivated by the inner satisfaction of getting a job done.

How to reach integrated people: Recognize these people publicly, but make certain they have tasks that interest them personally. For example, if you know someone on your team likes to do different things, ask her to develop a staff newspaper or put her in charge of a new project.

By observing your audience prior to your presentation, you can identify the different motivators before you begin. Armed with this information, you will be able to develop a presentation that will help them easily relate to what you are saying. If you are addressing a group of salespeople (outer-driven), you may want to incorporate some type of award system into the product introduction. Let them know that after your presentation they will be given a short test. Then reward the individual with the highest score. The issue is to be prepared and credible.

> *The issue is to be prepared and credible.*

Exercise

Now that you know how to identify the different personalities, take a few minutes to identify the personalities of the individuals in your audience, office or team.

Personality Type	Description	Person Identified
Needs-Driven	Sustainers/Survivors	_____
		_____
Inner-Directed	Internally Motivated	_____
		_____
Outer-Directed		_____
		_____
Achievers	Cheerleaders	_____
		_____
Belongers	Followers	_____
		_____
Integrated	Motivated in a number of ways	_____
		_____

2

Play to the Cheerleaders

During your presentation, look for the cheerleaders — the achievers that make up 20 percent of outer-directed individuals — and play to them. If you win over the cheerleaders, the belongers, who make up approximately 50 percent of your audience, tend to follow.

Interestingly, presenters tend to be directed and controlled by the negative personality types. Rather than being energized by the majority of people in the audience who are smiling and nodding in agreement, they are pulled to that one somber face, the one with the frown, the distracted look, the fingers drumming. They try to convince, cajole, persuade that one person, often to the detriment of the rest of the audience. It is usually a hopeless task. Don't waste energy focusing on the individual who is staring at you stone-faced! If you say something while looking at this person, you will lose your train of thought. You will spend so much time on that one person that you will miss out on others who are much more interested.

> *"Enthusiasm is like having two right hands."*
> Elbert Hubbard

Trainers/speakers must break this extremely debilitating habit of playing to the negative person by looking for the cheerleader early on, perhaps during the welcome, or as you handle introductions. Cheerleaders give you the encouragement and energy you need to make a great presentation. If you don't know your audience well enough to identify the cheerleaders ahead of time, it's easy to find them when making your presentation: They are the individuals in the crowd who are smiling with open, receptive faces.

During your presentation, keep coming back to the cheerleaders. They will make you feel good and give you the confidence to make your best presentation.

Being aware of and adapting your presentation to your audience ensures that every member of the group will feel like a winner. Remember, the most powerful motivators are those who positively enhance others' self-concepts.

What Your Audience Wants and Needs to Know

Once you know who your audience is, it is important for you to structure your presentation around what they want and need to know. Let's look at the following case study.

Bill has been asked by his boss to give a presentation to the customer relations department on answering the telephone. The company has received a number of complaints from customers, including:

- calls are not answered promptly
- callers are placed on hold for too long
- customer service reps have been rude

As the presenter, it is Bill's job to address these issues. These are things his audience *needs* to know. But Bill also must determine what his audience *wants* to know. For example, Bill *needs* to tell the customer service representatives that in order to meet customer expectations, they need to answer all calls within three rings. What they are going to *want* to know is **how** they can do that when they are on another call. Therefore, Bill *needs* to explain how the customer service representative can place a customer on hold and then answer a second line.

Bill also *needs* to explain to the customer service representatives that they should strive to get back to a customer on hold within one minute. The customer service representatives, however, will *want* to know how to do that. To address their question, Bill might suggest using an egg timer to help them know when one minute is up. He might also suggest that at the end of one minute the customer service representative explain to the customer that it is taking the rep longer than anticipated and offer to call the customer back. Also, Bill could allow the reps to brainstorm other ideas to solve the problem.

Bill *needs* to explain to the customer service representatives about the importance of being polite to customers. But what they will *want* to know is how to do that when a customer is hostile and is calling them names. Once again, Bill must address what the customer service representatives *want* to know. He can do this by explaining to them how to handle irate customers.

C A S E

S T U D Y

2

When you're making a presentation, there will be things that your audience *needs* to know and other things that they *want* to know. What they need to know is generally dictated by the need for the presentation. As a presenter, it is your job to determine what your audience wants to know and make sure you address that as well, usually early in the presentation. Complete the following worksheet. Determine what Bill's audience wants to know.

Needs Satisfaction Worksheet

What does the audience need to know? (WHAT)

What does the audience want to know? (WHY) (HOW)

What are the possible benefits of a successful meeting for this audience? ("What's in it for me — WIIFM?")

What questions might the audience have?

2

Needs Satisfaction

To ensure that you address your audience's needs, complete the previous Needs Satisfaction Worksheet every time you make a presentation.

In order for your presentation to be successful, it is important for you to determine what your audience wants to know as well as what they need to know. If you address only what they need to know, they will leave your presentation with many unanswered questions, and the possibilities are great they learned little about what they wanted to know.

Questions for Personal Development

2

1. What is the major emphasis of this chapter?

   _____
   _____
   _____
   _____

2. What are the most important things you learned from this chapter?

   _____
   _____
   _____
   _____

3. How can you apply what you learned to your current job?

   _____
   _____
   _____
   _____

4. How will you go about making these improvements?

   _____
   _____
   _____
   _____

5. How can you monitor improvement?

   _____
   _____
   _____
   _____

6. Summarize the changes you expect to see in yourself one year from now.

   _____
   _____
   _____

2

Summary

In preparing your presentation, it is important for you to know some basic information about your audience.

- How many people will you be addressing?

- Will your audience consist of superiors, peers, associates, special interest groups or a mix?

- What is the group's level of expertise?

- What are your basic expectations about your presentation?

- What are the expectations (wants) of your audience?

In this chapter you learned about four different audience motivators: needs-driven, inner-directed, outer-directed and integrated. You learned how to identify each type and the best way to deal with them.

When addressing any group, it's important to identify the cheerleaders and focus your efforts to them. Find the individual with the smiling, receptive face and pretend that you are making your presentation for that one person. The smiles and nods you receive from that one individual will motivate you to make the best presentation possible. It will certainly affect the reactions of at least 68 percent of the rest of the audience.

C HAPTER 3

Identifying Your Presentation Style

After identifying your audience, the next question to answer is how to keep them from becoming bored.

People make presentations based upon their own comfort zones. Though people don't generally have a single, pure style, all have preferences toward which they gravitate.

Knowing your own personal presentation style will help you in developing presentations. In this chapter you will identify your presentation style, learn how this information can be helpful to you and assess your current ability to give presentations.

What Kind of a Presenter Are You?

Think of a speaker who dazzled you. What were his characteristics? What did he do? Now, identify the worst presentation you ever encountered. What did the presenter do or not do? What were some of the speaker's characteristics? The chances are that your descriptions of best and worst fall into distinct categories.

Generally speaking, there are three different presentation styles. Following is a description of each.

1. **The Cool-Zone Presenter**. The cool-zone presenter captures the audience's attention with clear-headed persuasiveness. During this type of presentation, things are orderly and stay under control. Presenters are often on a specific mission and can marshal arguments with military precision. Presenters come across as secure in their knowledge with an undeniable intensity. They are most comfortable with a strong data base, drawing upon facts and figures to substantiate what is being presented.

Well-known cool-zone presenters are former Secretary of State Henry A. Kissinger, commentator William F. Buckley Jr., political analyst Jeane Kirkpatrick, former United States President George Bush and broadcast journalist Connie Chung. Adjectives that describe cool-zone presenters include analytical, logical, pragmatic, thoughtful, deliberate, rational, restrained, intellectual and insightful.

> *"Enthusiasm I rate ... even ahead of professional skill."*
> Sir Edward Victor Norton, Nobel prize for physics

2. **The Hot-Zone Presenter**. The hot-zone presenter can blow the roof off a building. This is the type of person that audiences either like or dislike, but no one ignores. Presentations are fast and furious, delivered often at a rapid rate of speech. A presenter pushes passions to the limits and runs on adrenaline. The pause, the raising and lowering of the voice, the body movements are all dramatic and enhance the points made. Well-known hot-zone presenters are former United States President Ronald Reagan, civil rights leader Jesse L. Jackson, radio commentator Paul Harvey, former British Prime Minister Margaret Thatcher, former congresswoman Barbara Jordan and television journalist Barbara Walters. Adjectives that describe hot-zone presenters are emotional, driven, surprising, instinctive, charismatic, creative, impulsive, daring and disjointed.

3. **The Dull-Zone Presenter.** The dull-zone presenter lacks the heat of the hot-zone presenter and the incisive edge of the cool-zone presenter. Dull-zone presenters are afraid to take risks; therefore, their presentations tend to be bland and boring. You've undoubtedly endured a dull-zone presenter sometime in your life. Adjectives that describe dull-zone presenters are cautious, traditional, accommodating, compromising, predictable, neutral, noncommittal, ambivalent and boring.

The dull zone is a safe place from which to present because it doesn't change much. It is bland and there is a minimal risk. The very absence of color suggests that it is a bland presentation, one easily forgotten. So many presenters operate from the dull zone that it appears to be the norm, the most desirable style of presentation. Few audience members will tell a presenter that he is boring. Rather, the audience members may vaguely suggest that they couldn't really relate, that the presenter didn't quite grasp the reality of their situation, etc. It is hard

It is hard to tell a presenter when he is really boring since the presentation engulfs them like a huge fogbank obscuring the scenery.

Every presenter operates in all these zones. A central tendency pulls toward one zone because it is comfortable and non-threatening to the presenter's self-image. The best are either in the cool or the hot zones. The tendency for many is to float or drift into the dull-zone periodically. This could be due to laziness, poor preparation, little feedback or fear. There is also variance in each zone. Many presenters go from the vivid and intense to a light, washed-out quality; they dull around the hard edges.

To determine what you are, what you would like to be and what you should be, consider each issue separately. Which style is best for you depends upon you, your audience and the industry. The one absolute certainty is "Do Not Linger in the Dull Zone."

Whether you are a top executive or a scientist, a salesperson or a support staffer, your success depends on your ability to deal with people. There is no one best style. What works best for you begins with knowing your strengths.

Thomas Huxley asked: "Who am I and what, if anything, can I do about it?" The answer is plenty, if you know and build on your strengths.

Should you aim your style toward the cool zone? Effective cool-zone presentations require a great deal of preparation. They require good memories for facts, figures and supportive data. Many executives prefer cool-zone presentations and are more comfortable with them, believing that feelings and emotions have no place in business. Audiences are more patient with this type of presentation and allow the presenters to build their cases. Generally, this is a more persuasive approach, but logic is not as engrossing as emotion. Nothing is wrong with a dash of drama, but the main points must be strong, accurate and totally factual.

The hot zone elicits a feeling of participation from audiences that is more emotional than intellectual. Reactions tend to be visceral because style is more outgoing, more personal. Hot-zone presentations tend to involve audiences more quickly. Important perceptions are formed on sight. Judgments are rendered swiftly, with seldom any middle ground being covered. The content is not the only message; rather, the presenter is an important part of the message. This is a high-risk, high-reward presentation with a lot of action.

Your success depends on your ability to deal with people.

The ideal is to have your presentation be a blend of hot and cool zones, avoiding the dull zone.

Are you in the dull zone without knowing it? Ask these questions to assess:

1. When practicing, do you get bored?
2. Does your portion of a program get cut or eliminated more often than others?
3. After presenting, do people stay to ask you questions?
4. During a rehearsal, do associates ignore you?
5. Do you get comments that are very general, non-specific and vague?
6. Do people squirm in their chairs or look at their watches as you present?
7. Do people nod out or have blank expressions on their faces when you present?
8. Is there a great deal of shuffling and lack of attention during your presentation?
9. Do you sense a very low energy level in the audience?

> *"What we've got here is a failure to communicate."*
> from Cool Hand Luke

If you answered "Yes" to many of these questions, you are definitely turning dull.

The first commandment of self-confidence is "to thine own self be true." However, if you are slipping toward dull, you may need to change some habits.

As a presenter, you will be most successful if you incorporate a combination of the cool- and hot-zone characteristics. Try to avoid the dull zone. It can be visited, but not for long. Audiences tend to lose interest quickly with dull-zone presenters. Following are some tips to help you stay stimulating.

1. **Don't tell me, show me**. Graphics, visuals or hand-outs make a presentation come to life. Use these whenever possible. For example, don't tell your audience how back injuries can be prevented on the job — show some proper lifting techniques and then have audience members practice while you observe.

2. **Avoid using lecterns or podiums**. There is nothing more boring than a speaker who never moves. Lecterns and podiums tend to tie down speakers to one spot.

3

3. **If appropriate, use two easels**. Using two easels will add some additional movement and interest to your presentation. Use one for display objectives and the other for results. It is effective to determine a purpose for each easel. For example, easel one can be for ideas; easel two for action statements. This helps give visual messages.

4. **Maintain constant eye contact.** A good standard is never to break eye contact with your audience for more than 10 seconds. If you do, people check out. Practice making eye contact for three to five seconds with individuals, then making eye contact with another side of the room.

5. **Glance at your visuals, don't study them.** Your visual materials should be a trigger or reinforcer of your presentation content, not a crutch. Glance at them to direct your audience's attention to the visuals and ensure they are correct, and then look back immediately at the audience.

6. **Be yourself**. Audiences can spot a phony a mile away. Develop your own style and work on perfecting it. Don't try to imitate another speaker.

7. **Don't script your speech.** If you've ever been in a presentation where the speaker read his speech, you know how deadly this can be. If you create good notes and practice your presentation thoroughly, you won't have any problem making a presentation without a script.

> *Be yourself.*
> *Audiences can spot a*
> *phony a mile away.*

Presentation Style Assessment

What kind of a presenter are you? You may be a hot-, cool- or dull-zone presenter, or you may be a combination of two or even all three types. To find out what kind of a presenter you are, take the Social Style Assessment quiz on the following pages. This is not a personality test. After you have completed the assessment, total the number of checks you have in each column and record them at the end.

Social Style Assessment

Check Appropriate Answer
1   2   3   4

1. At a party, do you talk to:
    a. Many people, including strangers? ☐
    b. A few people known to you?   ☐

2. Do you make selections:
    a. Carefully?   ☐
    b. Somewhat impulsively?   ☐

3. Before making a phone call, do you:
    a. Rarely think about the details? ☐
    b. Rehearse what you'll say?   ☐

4. Do you place more emphasis on:
    a. The definite?   ☐
    b. The possible?   ☐

5. Do you prefer:
    a. Many friends with brief contact? ☐
    b. Few friends with lengthy contact?   ☐

6. Are you more:
    a. Serious and determined?   ☐
    b. Easygoing?   ☐

7. Choose one from each pair of words
    that best describes you:
    a. Social   ☐
    b. Territorial   ☐

    a. Settled   ☐
    b. Pending   ☐

    a. Expend   ☐
    b. Conserve   ☐

    a. Planner   ☐
    b. Adapter   ☐

3

		Check Appropriate Answer			
		1	2	3	4
a.	Broad	☐			
b.	Deep		☐		
a.	Fixed			☐	
b.	Flexible				☐
a.	Extensive	☐			
b.	Intensive		☐		
a.	Decisive			☐	
b.	Tentative				☐
a.	Interactive	☐			
b.	Concentrated		☐		
a.	Closed			☐	
b.	Open-ended				☐

8. Do you:
   a. Hurry to answer the phone first? ☐
   b. Hope someone else will answer? ☐

9. Are you more:
   a. Deliberate than spontaneous? ☐
   b. Spontaneous than deliberate? ☐

10. Are you:
    a. Easy to approach? ☐
    b. Somewhat reserved? ☐

11. Are you more:
    a. Routine than whimsical? ☐
    b. Whimsical than routine? ☐

12. At parties do you:
    a. Stay late with increasing energy? ☐
    b. Leave early with decreased energy? ☐

Check Appropriate Answer

	1	2	3	4

13. Does it bother you more having things:
    a. Incomplete?
    b. Complete?

14. Do you:
    a. Anticipate conversation?
    b. Wait to be approached?

15. In your daily schedule do you:
    a. Seek order?
    b. Take things as they come?

16. Do changes in daily events:
    a. Stimulate and energize you?
    b. Tax your reserves?

17. Are you more comfortable:
    a. After a decision?
    b. Before a decision?

18. Which saying best typifies you
    in each word pair:
    a. Let's talk.
    b. Let me think about it.

    a. Deadline!
    b. What deadline?

19. Do you:
    a. Overstate something to make a point?
    b. Understate something to be sure?

20. Which best typifies you?
    a. Get the show on the road!
    b. Let's wait and see.

TOTALS

What the Social Style Assessment Says About You

3

The previous test was developed to help you understand your own personal style so that you can utilize it most fully during your presentations. There are no right or wrong answers.

Look at your totals in columns one and two. If you have more checks in column one, you are an extrovert. If you have more checks in column two, you are an introvert. Now look at the totals in columns three and four. If you have more checks in column three, you are a judger. If you have more checks in column four, you are a perceiver. These are just tendencies; there are always exceptions.

What does all this mean? Following is a description of each characteristic.

An extrovert tends to be outgoing and persuasive.

- **Extrovert**: During a presentation, an extrovert tends to be outgoing and persuasive. Although being outgoing and persuasive are positive characteristics, as an extrovert you have to be careful not to steamroll your audience. Extroverts tend to be hot-zone presenters, who must be careful or they come across as hot air. Extrovert strengths include being supportive and easygoing. Some weaknesses include being confrontational, permissive or aggressive.

- **Introvert**: Introverts are more introspective. They tend to prefer their own company and may be perceived as somewhat dull. If you are an introvert, it is important for you to find ways to liven up your presentations. Introverts at their best tend to be cool-zone presenters, but they can slip into flat facts and monotone information that's of interest only to them, the dull zone. The strengths of an introvert include being precise and systematic, while weaknesses include being nitpicky and inflexible.

- **Judger**: If you are a judger, you are decisive and fixed when giving a presentation. You will probably say things such as, "This is the way it has to be done." Judgers tend

3

to be cool-zone presenters, unless they hook into emotional issues. They then become hot-zone speakers. Strengths of a judger include being enthusiastic and imaginative. If you overextend this style, you may become overbearing and unrealistic.

- **Perceiver**: If you are a perceiver, you are probably tentative and flexible. When making a presentation, you will say things such as, "This is the way it should work unless someone has a better idea." The perceiver's flexibility can open the door to the cool zone or hot zone by reading and meeting audience need. The perceiver can be determined and open; yet, if overextended, he can become dominating and unfriendly.

The preferences above center around two variables: how you relate to people and how you make decisions.

Presentation success is based on behaviors, and behaviors are adaptable, controllable. After you assess the situation and the audience, you can decide which style works best for you, adapting your own behaviors to conform to your audience.

The most powerful influence on one's life is how we view ourselves. Self-knowledge is the starting point for effective presentations and skill-building. Are you the presenter you want to be?

Exercise

Complete the exercise below to learn more about how you can improve your natural presentation style.

What kind of presenter are you?

hot-zone _____ cool-zone _____ dull-zone _____

What can you do to stay in the hot and cool zones?

_____

_____

_____

What can you do to stay out of the dull zone?

_____

_____

_____

Which are you, an extrovert or introvert? _____

If you are an extrovert, what kinds of precautions can you take to make sure you don't steamroll your audience?

_____

_____

If you are an introvert, what can you do to liven up your presentations?

_____

_____

_____

Which are you, a judger or perceiver? _____

If you are a judger, what steps can you take to be more flexible?

_____

_____

If you are a perceiver, how can you be more decisive?

_____

_____

Assessing Your Current Ability

Assessing your current ability to make presentations will help you identify your strengths and weaknesses and determine areas for improvement.

To assess your current presentation skills, take the following Self-Assessment Survey. Answer each item by checking under the spaces for *often, sometimes* or *seldom* in response to each statement. There are no right or wrong answers. The best answer is your honest answer.

Self-Assessment Survey

	Often	Sometimes	Seldom
1. I schedule time on my calendar to prepare for presentations.	☐	☐	☐
2. I plan only essential presentations whose purposes cannot be achieved in other ways.	☐	☐	☐
3. I alert those attending about the presentation and give them a schedule or outline at least five working days in advance.	☐	☐	☐
4. I plan for my audience's attention span.	☐	☐	☐
5. I prepare the overheads, documentation and other materials I need for my presentation well ahead of time.	☐	☐	☐

	Often	Sometimes	Seldom
6. Before my presentation I visit the room where it will be held and check the equipment I will use.	☐	☐	☐
7. I rehearse my presentation several times until I feel comfortable with the material.	☐	☐	☐
8. I complete an audience analysis before the presentation.	☐	☐	☐
9. I incorporate visual aids into my presentation.	☐	☐	☐
10. I involve participants within the first few minutes of my presentation.	☐	☐	☐
11. I evaluate the process and my performance after each presentation.	☐	☐	☐

If you answered *often* to more than half of the items in the Self-Assessment Survey, you currently prepare for presentations better than do your peers. If you answered *sometimes* or *seldom* more than half of the time, there is some room for improvement. But don't worry. All the items covered in the survey will be discussed in future chapters. Soon you'll feel more confident and competent when making presentations.

3

Questions for Personal Development

1.   What is the major emphasis of this chapter?

_____
_____
_____
_____

2.   What are the most important things you learned from this chapter?

_____
_____
_____
_____

3.   How can you apply what you learned to your current job?

_____
_____
_____
_____

4.   How will you go about making these improvements?

_____
_____
_____
_____

5.   How can you monitor improvement?

_____
_____
_____
_____

6.   Summarize the changes you expect to see in yourself one year from now.

_____
_____
_____
_____

Summary

3

In this chapter you learned what your personal presentation style is. Armed with that information, you can design presentations that build on your strengths. In making presentations, you can avoid the dull zone by:

• Showing your audience what you tell them

• Avoiding lecterns and podiums

• Using two easels

• Maintaining constant eye contact

• Glancing at your visual aids

• Being yourself

• Presenting, not reading, your material

> *"Do not be awestruck by people and try to copy ... Nobody can be you as efficiently as you can."*
> Norman Vincent Peale

You also assessed your current presentation ability by taking the Self-Assessment Survey. This survey shows the amount of preparation involved in making any presentation. No matter how well a presenter knows his topic, if the details are left to chance, the presentation may be a failure.

In summary, know who you are. Let who you are become your primary presentation style.

The best speakers are themselves at their best.

3

CHAPTER 4

Preparation and Practice

Now that you have defined your audience and identified your own personal presentation style, it's time to focus on the most important part of your presentation — the preparation and practice. In this chapter, you will learn how to bring together all of your material to ensure that you make the best presentation possible. You also will learn some tips for rehearsing your presentation.

> *"Luck is a very good word if you put a P before it."*
> Anonymous

Putting It All Together

Before you can begin to structure your presentation, you must first complete several important steps. Following is an explanation of each.

- **Clarify your topic**. Make sure you know exactly what it is you will be speaking about. If someone else has asked you to make the presentation, go back to that individual to make sure you understand the topic. For example, if your boss has asked you to make a presentation on the company's newest products, ask for clarification about which products should be discussed. Also, find out the main point your boss expects you to get across to the audience. Are you going to present the benefits of the new products or demonstrate how they work?

- **Identify your theme**. This is the message around which you will weave your content, the thread that connects all

4

Identify what's interesting, attention-getting and unusual about your topic.

your points. A theme is pivotal for every topic and subpoint. You should be able to write your theme on the back of a business card. It must be that clear and succinct.

- **Research your topic**. As discussed earlier, before making a presentation you must be familiar with your topic. Now is the time to do any additional research that's needed and to organize your data.

Some ways to research:
- talk to customers
- talk to users
- talk with department personnel and associates
- review annual reports, company information
- review information in the library
- read competitors' reports
- read current magazine articles on the topic
- skim books written in the last three years on the topic

Identify what's interesting, attention-getting, beneficial and unusual about your topic.

- **Identify appropriate visuals**. As you gather information, ask yourself what you have that would make your point visually. For example, if you are discussing sales figures, you might want to include graphs and charts to better illustrate your points. If you are explaining the areas of the country your company currently serves, a map of the United States might be helpful. Also consider using slides or a brief videotape if they are available and applicable to your topic.

Compiling an Agenda

Developing an agenda will help you organize your presentation, as well as help attendees schedule their time. Be sure to include the time the presentation will start, the time it will end and when specific topics will be discussed. An agenda does not need to be long or extremely detailed. Note the simplicity of the examples on the following pages, yet how they provide all the necessary details.

4

SAMPLE AGENDA

Sales Presentation
Monday, September 20, 1994
Jim Smith

8 - 8:30 a.m.	Continental breakfast
8:30 - 9 a.m.	Introduction of new products
9 - 9:30 a.m.	Demonstration of new products
9:30 - 10:15 a.m.	Tips on selling new products
10:15 - 10:30 a.m.	Break
10:30 - 11:30 a.m.	Ways to increase your customer list
11:30 - Noon	Questions and answers

SAMPLE AGENDA
Technical Report Product Liability

20-Minute Presentation
- Why product liability is a concern for the company
- Components of the threat
- How it has been addressed in the past
- How this relates to your department
- Questions

"I'm working so hard on my time management that I don't get anything done."
Anonymous

SAMPLE AGENDA

60-Minute Presentation to Board of Directors on the financial status of the company

- Current state of affairs
- Challenges to the industry
- Strengths of company's financial position
- Areas of growth
- Issues of concern
- Proposal to strengthen position during next six months

Distribute your agenda at least five working days in advance so that attendees can schedule their time appropriately.

> *"It is a bad plan that admits of no modification."*
> Publilius Syrus

4

ABC Company Quarterly Meeting
June 1, 1994

Purpose: To publicly recognize 1993 "Outstanding Associates" award recipients and announce 1994 award criteria and nomination procedure

Agenda:
8:30-8:45 a.m.	Welcome and introductions
8:45-10:45 a.m.	Presentation of awards
10:45-11:15 a.m.	Break
11:15-12:15 p.m.	1994 award criteria and nomination process
12:15-12:30 p.m.	Wrap-up

Limit: 4 hours; 8:30 am - 12:30 pm

XYZ Company Annual Meeting
January 1, 1994

Purpose: To review 1993 performance, by department, and develop 1994 goals, objectives and strategies

Attendees: A. Smith, J. Jones, C. Miller, T. Brown

Agenda:
• Welcome and introductions	J. Jones
• Review of previous meeting minutes	A. Smith
• Discussion of 1994 goals and objectives	J. Jones
• Break-out sessions	All
• Presentation of departmental goals	All
• Assign action items	C. Miller

Limit: 8 hours; 8 a.m. - 5 p.m.

Location: The Towers Hotel
23rd Street and NW Expressway
Comanche Ballroom

Structuring Your Thoughts

4

Once you have gathered all the information you need for your presentation, you need to determine how to present the material to your audience. Basically, there are three methods you can use: deductive, inductive or a combination of the two.

You may have to step out of your comfort zone and present your argument in a manner that is unfamiliar to you, yet is familiar to the audience. This could require some imaginative empathizing with your audience. If you are trying to convince a group of writers, think about the challenges they face or how they organize their work. If you are presenting to salespeople, think about how they must be able to accept rejection. If you are speaking with scientists, concentrate on logic and order. If you are working with bankers, visit your own banker, learn the language and her business. Review each method below and determine which will work best for you.

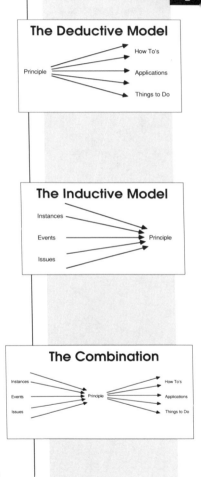

1. **Deductive**. This type of presentation is structured in a lecture format. It is the easiest to present. You simply take your ideas and/or principles and pass them on to your audience. You then tell your audience what to do or how to use the information you just presented. The deductive method leaves little opportunity for questions and answers. For example, Mary is going to give a presentation on ways to increase her company's profits. Using this model, she would say to her audience, "The best way for us to increase our profits is to do the following ..." This is a subtraction method of presenting. It looks at the entire form, then divides it into pieces, as a scientist might. Chemists are actually testing out a principle when they use this method. It presents the whole first and then the pieces. The majority of the general public is deductive in preference.

2. **Inductive**. This type of presentation provides a little more flexibility. It is good to use when you want group participation. In this format, you help the audience reach a conclusion or a consensus based on the dialogue with your audience. You present instances, events or issues and then ask the group to help you determine the principle. In the previous example, if Mary were using the inductive model she would say, "Our goal today is to determine ways

to increase profits. Does anyone have any thoughts on that?" Based on what the group said, an agreement would be reached on the best way to increase profits. A creative, innovative person is likely to prefer the inductive method. This method starts with the pieces and builds a case. Many scientists, true to their discipline, will build a presentation from clues and innuendos, conduct research, and lastly make their recommendation.

The combination method is like a piece of symphonic music ... it explodes, it thins, it weaves ...

3. **Combination**. This method takes longer and involves greater audience participation. You discuss an idea, reach a conclusion and then tell your audience what to do based on the group consensus. In this method, you suggest instances, events or issues and ask your audience to help you determine the principle. Based on the information you gather, you tell your audience how to proceed. If Mary were using the combination model, she would say, "Our goal today is to determine ways to increase profits. Does anyone have any thoughts on that?" The group would then discuss the issue, make some suggestions and come to a conclusion. Mary would then say, "Based on what we've agreed to, this is what we will do to increase profits." Some participants might find the inductive method tedious. They may want the presenter to get to the point quickly. As the presenter begins to lay the groundwork, explain the situation and build the case, they might interrupt loudly, "What's the bottom line? Do we or don't we?" This type of person will not listen until she is first assured it is worth the time. The combination method is like a piece of symphonic music. Like "Bolero" by Maurice Ravel, it explodes, it thins, it weaves, first one way, and then the other.

Before you actually begin to prepare the content of your presentation, using one of these methods, you need to research your subject matter. Use the following checklist to ensure that you have taken all the necessary steps.

Checklist

1. I have clarified my topic.

I will be speaking about _____.

My audience will expect to learn _____.

2. I have researched my topic.

I have researched my topic by _____.

I need additional information on the following:

_____

_____

_____

3. I have identified visual aids needed for my presentation.

I have planned visuals to illustrate the following points of my presentation:

_____

_____

_____

4. I have completed my agenda.

I will distribute my agenda on (date)_____.
(at least five working days before presentation)

5. I have determined which method I will use to make my presentation:

☐ Deductive

☐ Inductive

☐ Combination

Once you have determined the best method to use when making your presentation, it's time to develop the outline.

Developing an Outline

An outline helps you organize your thoughts visually.

The following diagram will help you develop an outline of your presentation. This outline will help you organize your thoughts visually.

The Three Triangle Outline is very similar to a method that journalists use when writing news articles. It's called the inverted pyramid. Using this method, the most important points are placed at the beginning of the article and are followed in descending order by the least important. In this way, editors can easily shorten an article by eliminating information from the bottom up.

The Three Triangle Outline can be used in the same way by presenters. This outline allows you to develop your presentation so that you can cut out portions if time runs short, starting at the bottom of each triangle. By organizing your presentation in this manner, you are assured of making your most important points, even if you run short on time or are given less time than you were originally told you would have.

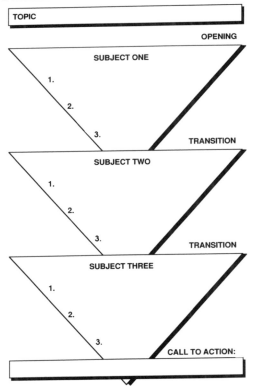

THREE TRIANGLE OUTLINE

TOPIC

OPENING

SUBJECT ONE
1.
2.
3.

TRANSITION

SUBJECT TWO
1.
2.
3.

TRANSITION

SUBJECT THREE
1.
2.
3.

CALL TO ACTION:

• *SAMPLE* •
THREE TRIANGLE OUTLINE

| TOPIC | Producing Newsletters |

OPENING

SUBJECT ONE
WHY PRODUCE A NEWSLETTER?
1. To generate business

2. To keep clients informed

3. To advertise
   our products

TRANSITION

SUBJECT TWO
HOW TO PRODUCE A NEWSLETTER
1. Gather info

2. Write copy/design format

3. Work with the
   printer

TRANSITION

SUBJECT THREE
DISTRIBUTING NEWSLETTER
1. Compile mailing list

2. Check postal regulations

3. Work with a
   mail house

CALL TO ACTION:

4

The triangular design helps you follow Edward R. Murrow's advice: "Tell 'em what you're going to tell them. Tell them. Tell them what you told them." It is logical, concise and appropriate for any subject or audience, and it helps you focus on what is *"must know."*

Let's examine the Three Triangle Outline on the next page a little closer. First, notice that there is space to write your topic at the top of the outline. Secondly, note that each of the three triangles represents the three key points of your speech:

- The top triangle is your most compelling point.
- The second is the body.
- The third leads toward the close.

At the top of each triangle is a space for you to write the subject of each part of your presentation. Within each triangle, write the points you want to make. You can have as many as five points. The most important point should be number one. When writing in each triangle, use this guide to know what to write down for each point.

Point 1.   What you **must** say
Point 2.   What you **should** say
Point 3.   What you **could** say
Point 4.   What you **might** say
Point 5.   What you'll say *if you have time*

Think of your outline as a map — a tool to help you get from point to point. This outline should guide you through your presentation. You won't read from it, but it will let you know what you've covered and what comes next.

Exercise

Imagine that you are asked to make a presentation about yourself. Using the Three Triangle Outline method just described, develop an outline that would help you present yourself to another person. (If you have questions, refer to the sample Three Triangle Outline.)

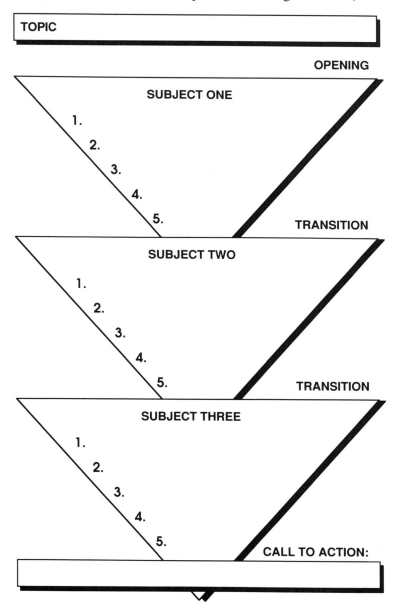

TOPIC

OPENING

SUBJECT ONE

1.
2.
3.
4.
5.

TRANSITION

SUBJECT TWO

1.
2.
3.
4.
5.

TRANSITION

SUBJECT THREE

1.
2.
3.
4.
5.

CALL TO ACTION:

In planning any presentation, keep the following tips in mind.

*Law of Primacy:
People remember
most what they
hear first.*

- Know what is most important and say it.

- Know what your audience needs to hear and say it. (Your Audience Analysis will help.)

- Include a strong opening and a strong close for your presentation. People tend to remember most what they hear first and they remember best what they hear last. For example, you might open a presentation to a group of salespeople by saying, "Today I'm going to show you how you can increase your commissions by 40 percent." Or, you might close the presentation by saying, "The secret to your success is you. If you begin to incorporate at your your office this afternoon what you learned today, you're bound to see a remarkable increase in sales."

- The most important times in a presentation are:

  - the first five minutes, at which time you make your initial impression on the audience members
  - the next 15 minutes, as they assess your worth and that of the program
  - the last 20 minutes, when they finalize their evaluation of you and the presentation

*Law of Recency:
People remember
best what they
hear last.*

Think of your presentation in three parts: your introduction, which is approximately 10 to 15 percent of your entire presentation; the body of your presentation, which consists of approximately 70 percent of content; and the conclusion, which is five to 10 percent of the total presentation. The modular outline design can assist you in developing these three distinct parts, with the body requiring a triangle module for each 20-minute segment.

The Opening

With regard to the opening, **CAP** your remarks. In this part of your presentation, three points are essential:

First: Capture attention by noting common ground, a point of interest or a hook.

Second: Authenticate the value of what you say by showing "What's in it for me?" to the participants.

Third: Prove your credibility and credentials and convince them of your right to speak.

"What's in it for me?"

4

You can capture attention through a variety of ways: a formal definition of the subject matter, a poem, current event, statistics, rhetorical questions, historical references, quotes, visuals, humor, startling facts, personal experiences and relevant situations. This is the time to identify and address any potential problems, and thus disarm the audience. If the visibility of audio/visuals is poor, if the temperature is proving a challenge, if expectations are other than what is possible, note these at the beginning, after establishing your credibility, and note their lack of importance with regard to the true purpose and value of the presentation.

Authenticating your materials from the onset is critical. It tells the listener whether they should invest their time and energy listening to you. It's during your authentication time that the listeners say to themselves, "This is really what I need," or "This speaker really knows where I have problems." The process of authenticating your materials generates "buy-in" to your ideas and concepts. Without an appeal to *what's in it for the listener* during the opening, the chances are great they'll leave your session. They may not check out physically, but if you don't authenticate your message by addressing what they will get out of the presentation, the chances are good they'll leave mentally.

One aspect of authenticating your materials and the third aspect of creating a positive opening is authenticating your credentials. Speaker credibility must be established during the opening. Selling one's credentials cannot be long, it cannot appear boastful, but it must be done clearly and accurately, justifying why a listener should pay attention. Credentials include where the speaker has been, what she has done and what experiences have generated this expertise. This is not the time to be overly self-revealing, but it is the time to stand on your laurels as the speaker. The opening can leave no doubt about whether the speaker has a right to talk on the subject being presented.

Transitions

Once you have an outline of your presentation, you need to add transitions. Transitions can be stories, illustrations, anecdotes or jokes. Write these to the side of each triangle.

A transition should be something that helps you do just that: move smoothly between subjects. For example, in the exercise where you described yourself, an example of a transition would be, "Flunking math in elementary school was traumatic for me. That experience taught me a great deal about life. It taught me to be strong and learn from my mistakes. Learning from my mistakes is what got me in the job I'm in today."

Transition Worksheet

#1 Select a key concept, issue or problem that must be
    illuminated. _____

#2 Identify all the features associated with this subject and
    a benefit for each.

Feature   Benefit

• _____   • _____
• _____   • _____
• _____   • _____
• _____   • _____
• _____   • _____

#3 Target your message. If you had time for only one
    feature and benefit, on which one would you focus?

    _____

#4 Expand the benefit, applying it to as many issues as
    possible.

#5 Build your bridges. Where do you have experiences,
    issues or interesting points that "link" the concept to
    your audience?

#6 Illustrate your point ...

Call to Action

You write your call for action at the bottom of the Three Triangle Outline. This is what you want your audience to do after hearing your presentation. If you have given a presentation to a group of salespeople about a particular product, your call to action might be, "Using what you learned today, go out there and sell!"

For the close, you must **MOVE** your audience. The close must result in action — something the audience must do. Although the presentation ends, the presentation does not end successfully until the audience members complete what they are to do. This consists of four points:

For the close, you must move your audience.

4

First: Motivate them to agree with, support and do whatever your theme requires.

Second: Orient them to what you have done and what they can now do.

Third: Validate everything you said as it relates to their specific needs.

Fourth: Excite them through your call to action.

Exercise

Transitions make your presentation flow. Go back to the exercise about presenting yourself to another person and write an opening and two transitions. Be sure to include your call to action at the bottom.

Opening _____
_____
_____
_____
_____
_____

Transition #1 _____
_____
_____
_____
_____
_____

Transition #2 _____
_____
_____
_____
_____
_____

Call to Action _____
_____
_____
_____
_____

Frame Every Speech and Presentation

When a frame is placed around a picture, it draws attention to the subject matter and filters the images outside the frame. Framing is a tool of perspective, a tool for presenting your "Key Concepts."

Like a picture frame, every presentation must have four sides to it in order for it to have meaning and impact with an audience.

Framing Key Concepts: _____

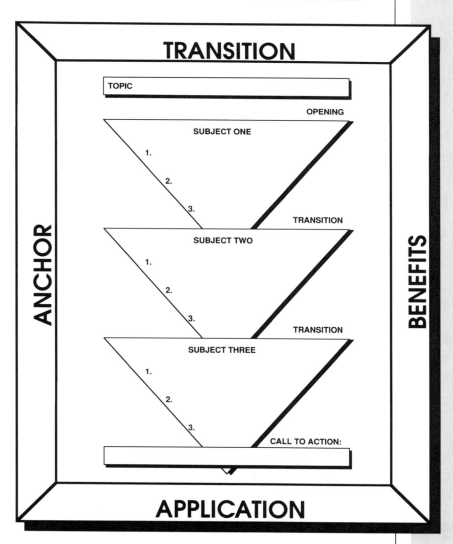

The Body

The body of any presentation includes the main points in the Three Triangle Outline. Incorporated into the body, at 10-12 minute "framed" intervals, are the transitions, anchors, benefits and applications. Remember: "Summarize or Exercise" your content every 10-12 minutes to maximize audience attention span.

A transition is a link between your points and topics.

- **Transition: A transition is a link or a segue between your points and topics.** It relates what you *are* saying with what you *were* saying and to what you *will* say. Transitions make your presentation logical and create flow. A transition can consist of an attention-grabber, a story, a surprise or a pick-up on the last words said. An example of a transition at the beginning of a presentation is:

> "Welcome, my name is Mary Hubert and I would like to tell you a story." Or, an example for a presentation to a CEO announcing a new product: "I am pleased to discuss with you the new drug we have developed, which will have immediate success in the pharmaceutical industry."

Some key questions and thoughts to help build a transition include:

- What is interesting or exciting about this concept?
- How can I relate this concept to my audience immediately?
- Does this "key concept" relate to a story or example the audience knows?

Dos and Don'ts When Illustrating Your Message

<u>Do</u>	<u>Don't</u>
1. Illustrate what has been said	1. Introduce new information
2. Do talk to person/user about how this will help her	2. Don't talk about the example
3. Do focus on benefit	3. Don't focus on features
4. Do create value	4. Don't get caught in excess details
5. Do use the familiar	5. Don't get too creative

- **Anchor**: An anchor is required for every topic or issue. An anchor acts like a hook; it links the speech or presentation into the emotions. This can be done through a statistic, a story, a joke or an analogy. It grabs attention and gives the listener something with which to remember the point being made. Anchors are generally "charged" with emotion and impact.

  The American Lung Association illustrated the difficulty and the benefit of anchoring key concepts when they attempted to impress the public with the seriousness of smoking-related diseases. They had little support, though they had very impressive statistics. Every day nearly 1,000 people die prematurely from smoking-related diseases. One thousand people a day, 365,000 a year — no better statistics for an anti-smoking campaign. Finally, they identified the perfect anchor: 1,000 deaths a day could be compared to two fully loaded jumbo jets colliding over your home every day, killing all passengers. When the statistics were "anchored" in this fashion, the consequences became real for the reader.

Anchors are generally charged with emotion and impact.

Some key questions to help anchor your message are:
- Where is the emotional, personal and psychological pressure point? Can I hit it?
- How will this audience respond at a "gut level"?
- What can I say that causes a person to link or bond with my idea?
- Do I have a story, illustration, example or statistic that hits my audience with impact?
- If my audience left for a fire drill right after my anchor, would they remember it? And would they want to return?
- Have I paid attention to the four types of anchors?
  — Visual (Sight)
  — Verbal (Sound)
  — Tactile (Touch)
  — Kinesthetic (Feeling)

4

- **Benefits**. The benefits address the "what's-in-it-for-me?" concern that is fundamental to every participant. The benefit must be introduced immediately and reiterated throughout your presentation.

    Example: A research director, making a presentation at an annual budget review, needed to convince the audience that research is important. He began by saying, "One of our researchers developed a substitute for a high-priced ingredient in a food product that saved the brand over $9 million per year. While we may never be a profit center, this department will continue to contribute to the company's bottom line."

People "buy" what you say when the presentation identifies the benefits to your audience. Benefits are created by answering these questions:

- "What's in it for me?"
- Will this concept ...
    make my life easier?
    make my life better?
    make me more money?
    save me money?
    save me time?

- **Application:** This is the "how to" information that's required in every presentation. The application should provide an answer to the question, "How do I use what you have just presented?"

    An example of this can be seen in a presentation to a real estate investment organization, concerning the hazards in the present marketplace. After an overview, which transitioned the listeners into the presentation, the speaker presented the analogy of an amber light. Traffic lights are an investment industry cliché, one easily recognized by the audience. The speaker noted that "in today's business environment, the light was neither red nor green, but was,

"Talk to a man about himself and he will listen for hours."
Benjamin Disraeli

4

in fact, amber, one that told us to proceed with extreme caution." The presentation then went on to outline what the issues were, how to address them, and their relevance to the audience. Specific principles were noted that were important for the audience to adhere to. "How tos" were laid out numerically with easy-to-follow instructions. It's important that people act on what you say. An effective application can be designed by answering these questions:

- How can this concept be used on the job?
- Can you state specific examples of where and when to apply this concept?

It's important that people act on what you say.

4

By *framing* all ideas around the presentation's central theme and organizing the opening, body and close in individual frames, you are guaranteed your audience will stay with you and see the merits of your presentation.

4

Framing Example:
Marketing a new product to a customer group

TRANSITION:

"There are a lot of products out there for you to choose from that meet the needs of your company. Certainly, there are a lot of less costly tires for your equipment, just as there are some that are more expensive. The tires my company produces, however, work and keep working.

ANCHOR:

An associate of mine likes to tell the story of Henry Ford taking a ride in the English countryside and coming upon a stalled car. Looking under the hood were a group of people who appeared to have been there for some time. Ford offered his assistance, went over to take a look and returned to his vehicle. He obtained a tool, returned to the stalled car, gave a certain piece of equipment a few taps and the motor started up. The people he assisted were elated and asked how much they could pay for his services. Ford replied: 100 pounds. The people were astounded and asked how he could ask so much for a few taps of a tool. Ford answered that two pounds were for the tapping and 98 pounds were for knowing where to tap. In my tire company, knowing exactly what and how to produce tires is what makes our product superior.

BENEFIT:

I have noted several uses for the tires my company can offer you. Let me tell you how they can be useful in your business. First, by offering these tires with your product, you can track the longer life of the product. Second, by including this feature in your store ads, you can demonstrate the durability of the entire unit.

APPLICATION:

To summarize, you can increase your market three-fold, add value and longevity to your product and have a market advantage over the competition. In short, with these tires you can expect profit increases of 118 percent over a six-month period. Let me illustrate ..."

Framing Example

TRANSITION:
- mention other sources
- why you should do business with my company

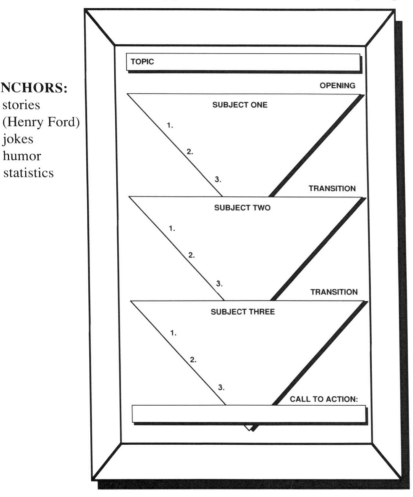

ANCHORS:
- stories (Henry Ford)
- jokes
- humor
- statistics

BENEFITS:
- longer product (tire) life
- demonstrated durability

APPLICATION/SUMMARY:
- increased profits (118 percent over 6-month time period)
- increased market share
- improved product perception

Framing Worksheet

Photocopy this page and use it whenever you are asked to make a presentation.

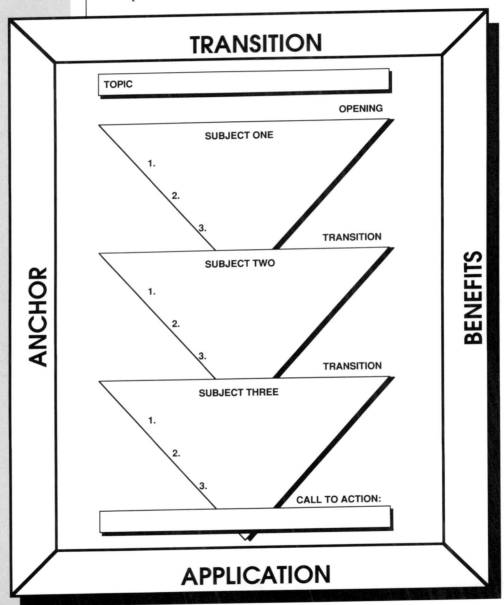

Review
Five Action Steps for Framing Your Thoughts

1. Develop a comprehensive presentation plan that pinpoints issues and desired outcomes.

2. Identify a theme for your session — the thread that connects all content pieces. A presentation must have one, and only one, theme.

3. Construct an organized outline of topics that allows the theme to flow logically from concept to concept.

4. Emphasize the three most important parts of training in:
    *   the first five minutes
    *   the next 15 minutes
    *   the last 20 minutes

5. Frame key concepts in 20-minute blocks of time:
    *   Transition — to carry subjects, link ideas through theme
    *   Anchor — to grab attention, draw participation and hook emotions
    *   Benefits — constantly noting in real world terms WIIFM
    *   Application — specific "how tos" for immediate gain

Remember to frame your concepts, and your presentation will have a much greater impact.

> *Frame your concepts, and your presentation will have a much greater impact.*

4

Storytelling

A story well-told will make any presentation stronger.

Principles of Storytelling

There is nothing more fun to listen to than a good story, and a story well-told will make any presentation stronger. Storytelling is not a gift, it's a learned skill — one that must be practiced, one that must develop as a presenter's style form. Storytelling must be tactical; a good story cannot be told unless there is an instructional purpose. There are three basic principles to every good story:

1. A good story always illustrates and supports materials that are already being taught. The story should not be the message.

2. Every story must have broad appeal. The listeners should be able to find themselves in the story.

3. The story should link images and concepts together. A well-told story will make the concept seem basic and, when used appropriately, a well-taught concept should make a story seem profound. The story and your message must be linked together.

Dos and Don'ts of Effective Storytelling

The effective storyteller follows the principles above. She also knows there are some things that hurt or help the stories she tells. Below are a list of the dos and don'ts of storytelling.

Don'ts:

If your story only entertains, don't use it.
If your story takes the listener nowhere, don't use it.
If your story must be explained, don't use it.
If a story puts down an identifiable individual (unless it's yourself), don't use it.
If a story cannot be encapsulated into 25 words, don't use it — it's too complex.

Dos:

Employ a simple story line. Stories with multiple themes are hard to follow and nearly impossible to tell well.

Have a small cast of characters. Although a great novelist can build interesting and engaging characters, when telling a story, your audience has a limited ability to hold numerous characters in mind. Limit the number of key characters to as few as possible, usually no more than four.

Stretch reality. Exaggeration helps the storyteller make two points:

- This is not real, but it supports what is real. This helps separate the story from the content.

- Exaggeration helps the person look for the message rather than trying to validate the substance of the story.

Rely on the familiar. Nothing will cause audience members to check out faster than if you tell a story about a movie they didn't see. But be careful. If the listeners know the story they will judge you on whether you told it as well as the last person they heard, and will likely miss the point you are making.

Limit the number of key characters to ... no more than four.

4

Characteristics of the Story

Every story has definable characteristics. It is to the presenter's advantage to understand and build on these characteristics. The first characteristic of an effective story is that the story has an obvious beginning and obvious ending. It is extremely hard for the listener to identify when a story starts and ends in many cases; as a result, the message is often lost in the story.

Telling too few stories is much better than too many. If you are going to err, make sure it is on the side of omission. Rarely will people say, "That was a good presentation, but there weren't any good stories." But they will say, "I wish the stories would stop and the speaker would just tell what is important."

The second characteristic of an effective story is that it is well placed. People remember stories. They are fun to listen to and the animation of the speaker telling a story is usually a relief from the predictable presentation of information. It's the responsibility of the speaker, however, to ensure that she tells the story and stops. Don't re-tell the story! The speaker must also live the story, breathing form and substance into it. Probably the most important aspect of orchestrating an effective story is to constantly remind yourself that it's your story; don't project it onto other people. The listeners must feel that they can protect themselves. Stories told about someone else or a story that gets its power by making fun of someone or something is a poor story.

How to Get Started as a Storyteller

Don't expect to stand in front of an audience the first time and tell a polished story. Storytelling takes time to develop. The effective storyteller must learn to use her voice, rate of speech and rhythm automatically. Getting started as a speaker means becoming a student of words and the way they are used. As a first step, read. Select writers who make a point and whose style appeals to you. Examples include: Will Rogers, Garrison Keillor, Mark Twain and Paul Harvey. Each of these writers makes a very clear statement through his story line.

Learn to listen to your voice and the voice of excellent storytellers. The storyteller's voice actually becomes a musical instrument playing a tune of entertainment. Tape record yourself telling stories. Once you've read a short story several times, the words become rote, but the impact of those words can be dramatic. This can be fun!

Pay attention to the stories that have worked throughout time. Stories and parables in the Bible, Aesop's fables, Grimm's fairy tales and the Disney stories all have a moral message, and many originally existed as oral stories designed to be told by a storyteller. It's also helpful to watch comedians and other professional speakers who make their living getting people to listen to their stories. Watch for bridges, introductions and transitions. How do they move their audiences from one point to the next? What technique is being employed to keep you involved in the story?

Rehearse stories you are very comfortable with and tell them

> *"Laughter can be more satisfying than honor, more precious than money ..."*
> Harriet Rochlin

4

many times in your mind. Once you can get from point to point without checking your notes, it's time to make the story yours by changing the impact with your voice and timing.

Last, but probably first in importance, become a student of storytelling. Learn how to watch for a storyline and how a character is developed in a very short time. Commercials are great examples of quick, but persuasive, messages built into a storyline. Make yourself step into the story, becoming one of the characters. This will help you identify emotions and reactions that might be perfect for teaching a concept.

Most stories carry many messages. A good storyteller knows that it's too time consuming to know a lot of stories. Instead, they learn two or three stories and then apply them to different situations. Good stories are recyclable!

Every good story relies on familiarity.

4

Mastering Storytelling — Four Essentials

#1 Every good story begins with a good storyteller who possesses the following speaking skills:
  A. Rhythm
  B. Flow
  C. Impact
  D. Timing

#2 Every good story:
  A. Relies on familiarity
  B. Employs a simple storyline
  C. Develops only a small cast of characters
  D. Stretches reality or exaggerates the obvious

#3 Storytelling success principles:

  A. Stories work best when they illustrate or support what is being taught.
  B. Stories work best when the listeners can find themselves in the story.
  C. Stories work best when the speaker makes application links for the listener.

#4   Storytellers' resources:

A. Fictional resources (To best use this resource, identify human dilemmas)
   - Aesop's Fables
   - Mother Goose stories
   - Grimm's fairy tales

B. Inspirational resources (To best use this resource, be motivational)
   - Sports heroes
   - Historical heroes
   - Society heroes

C. Dramatic resources (To best use this resource, be thematic)
   - Great literature
   - Movies

D. Personal events (To best use this resource, be emotional)
   - Childhood experiences
   - Life-changing situations

Practice ... makes your presentation shine.

Rehearsing Your Presentation

Once you have finished preparing your presentation, it's time to rehearse it. Practice is the part of preparation that makes your presentation shine. In fact, half of your preparation time should be used to practice your presentation. For example, if you spend three hours on research and two hours organizing your material, you should spend five hours rehearsing.

Before beginning your rehearsal, make sure that you have everything you will need, including visuals.

Then, follow these simple steps.

1. **Review your outline**. Check to make sure you've included all pertinent information. Color-code (highlight) your notes. Colors are often easier to spot than words or phrases as you make your presentation. For example:
    Yellow: slide or transparency
    Red: story or illustration
    Blue: optional material
    Green: general information, facts and stats
    Pink: ask a question
    Orange: take a break

2. **Talk through your presentation**. Sit in a comfortable chair and practice reciting what you are going to say, using your Three Triangle Outline.

3. **Tape record your presentation.** While standing, give your presentation out loud, using a tape recorder. After you have finished, listen to the tape. Consider the following questions:

    — Did you talk too fast or too slowly?
    — Do you have any speech mannerisms that could detract from your presentation? For example, do you repeatedly say, "um" or "OK"?
    — Did you use pauses effectively?
    — Was your volume too loud or too soft?
    — Did you come across as genuinely enthusiastic about your topic?
    — Did you pronounce words appropriately? Lazy speech suggests a lazy mind. Don't say things like *gonna* instead of *going to* or *coulda* instead of *could have*.

> *Lazy speech suggests a lazy mind.*

4. **Videotape your presentation or practice before a small group**. Give your presentation again, this time in front of a small group of people (even one person is fine) or use a videotape camera to record your presentation. If you make your presentation in front of people, ask them to critique it using the following questions. If you videotape it, critique yourself when you watch the tape.

— Did you stand straight and appear in control?
— Did your gesturing seem natural?
— Did your visuals complement your presentation or detract from it?
— Did you make regular eye contact with your audience?
— Did you smile occasionally and when appropriate? If you never smile, you could appear nervous. If you smile too much or at the wrong times, your audience will be confused.

5. **Correct specifics by giving your presentation several times before a mirror**. Practice correcting the criticisms from the audio- and videotapes. An excellent practice method is to give your presentation to a blank spot on a wall. This will prevent you from inadvertently adopting mannerisms.

6. **Use positive self-talk to tell yourself that you are adequately prepared and that you will do a good job**. For example, "I have really captured the essence of what I wanted to say," or "I came across as confident and well-prepared. My hard work has paid off."

7. **Visualize yourself giving a successful presentation.** This reinforces your preparation and will help you do your best.

Questions for Personal Development

4

1. Identify the major emphasis of this chapter.

    _____

    _____

    _____

2. What are the most important things you learned from this chapter?

    _____

    _____

    _____

3. How can you apply what you learned to your current job?

    _____

    _____

    _____

4. How will you go about making these improvements?

    _____

    _____

    _____

5. How can you monitor improvement?

    _____

    _____

    _____

6. Summarize the changes you expect to see in yourself one year from now.

    _____

    _____

    _____

Summary

Preparation is vital to a successful presentation. When preparing your presentation, there are several steps you must take:

1. Clarify your topic.

2. Research your topic.

3. Identify appropriate visual materials.

4. Develop an agenda and distribute it.

5. Structure your thoughts.

6. Develop an outline and color-code it.

7. Bring your outline together by framing your thoughts.

8. Rehearse your presentation until you feel comfortable.

In the next chapter you will learn about logistics and visual aids.

CHAPTER 5

Logistics and Visual Aids

Ideally, when preparing for your presentation, you begin with the theme, what you are going to say. This leads you to identify why this presentation is important, why the theme is relevant. You then proceed to "whom" your presentation is addressing and adapt the "what" and "why" around points relevant to the audience. This brings you to the "where," the "when" and the "how," or more precisely, the logistics.

Once you know what you are going to say, it's time to focus on the logistics of your presentation and your visual aids. Where are you going to conduct your presentation? How do you plan to arrange the seating? Will you use audio/visual equipment, overhead transparencies or charts?

In this chapter, you will learn to master the details that will ensure that you have a successful presentation.

Scheduling Your Presentation

If someone else has asked you to make the presentation, it is likely that the time and place are already scheduled. If not, it's up to you to find both a suitable time and place.

Consider these tips when scheduling the time and place for your presentation.

- **When will most of your audience be available?** After you have determined who your audience members are, you can determine the best time for them to attend. For example, if you are making a presentation for the sales department, check with the sales manager to see when most of the sales staff will be available.

In scheduling presentations or training sessions of two hours or less, keep these guidelines in mind:

Avoid Monday mornings and Friday afternoons.

— 8 to 10 a.m. is usually a good time because there are a minimum number of distractions. You can start before the audience's day begins.

— 10 a.m. to noon is considered peak time for brain activity. Presentations during this time period must be well-planned and action-oriented or the audience will feel that they have lost the most productive part of the day.

— Avoid scheduling immediately after lunch or late in the day. Most people find it difficult to concentrate at these times.

— Avoid Monday mornings and Friday afternoons. People will be concentrating on the weekend — either what they have planned or what they just did. They also need these times to prepare for the week's work ahead or to finish projects before the weekend.

• **If you are planning a presentation for more than two hours, consider refreshments or food.** Arrange for water and refreshments to be available. If it is going to be an all-day presentation, be sure to order lunch or schedule time for off-site lunches. If your participants are on their own for lunch, give them a list of nearby restaurants.

• **Be aware of the "hot times" of the business or industry.** For example, if you sell restaurant supplies, it's best to avoid breakfast, lunch and dinner rush hours; someone making presentations to hospital personnel should be aware of admitting and discharge times. Some companies reserve the last Thursday of every month for inventory counting. Many designate the first week of each quarter for financial report generation. These specifics should be noted in the agenda that is sent six to 12 days prior to the presentation.

- **Consider your audience when planning the length of your presentation**. If, for example, you are planning a presentation to a group of executives, it may be hard for them to schedule an entire day. However, if you have a lot of ground to cover in your presentation and feel that you need a full day, here are several options for flexibility:

    1. Inform the participants that they can stop in for those topics that have relevance to their needs, as noted on the agenda.
    2. Modularize the topics and present in sequential days (perhaps during breakfast meetings where the time is strictly adhered to).
    3. Condense the material to meet the schedules of the audience.
    4. Have pre-reads so that the information can be quickly covered.

It's imperative to develop an agenda and stick to it.

5

Developing an agenda and sticking to it is imperative. Remember to schedule breaks every couple of hours so your audience can move around, use the restrooms, check for phone messages and have refreshments.

Scheduling a Room

Depending on your presentation's content and audience, you may choose to conduct it at the office or at an outside location. An outside location is usually better if you need to limit interruptions. Either way, schedule the room well in advance and take time to evaluate it. Don't take someone's word over the phone that the space will work for your presentation.

If you are using audio/visual equipment, make certain the room has electrical outlets where you need them, and ask about bringing in or ordering the equipment that you need. You may have to pay hook-up fees for sound system output.

Visit the site prior to booking it so that you can confirm and adjust any specific requirements. Many conference rooms are ideal, according to the brochure of the hotel or convention center. Yet, a "beautiful garden room" might mean a tent in the garden; "few amenities" could mean only one toilet; "close to industrial center" could mean next to the railroad tracks with a train whistling past every three minutes; "decorative columns accentuating room" could mean pillars throughout, which make visibility impossible for two-thirds of the audience.

Remember, whatever can go wrong, will. "Prepare for the worst, plan on the best, and enjoy it all."

Make a list of the equipment you are going to need — easel, slide projector, screen, television monitor, etc. Reserve them well ahead of time and have a list of back-up vendors and places where you can order additional equipment should yours go awry.

MEETING PLANNER

Meeting Date: _____ Start Time: _____
Location: _____ End Time: _____

Chairperson: _____
Phone #: _____ Fax#: _____
Scribe: _____

Purpose: _____
Objective: _____
Agenda Completed? ❑ Yes ❑ No

ATTENDEES:

Name	Phone	Notified?	Confirmed?
_____	_____	❑ Y ❑ N	❑ Y ❑ N
_____	_____	❑ Y ❑ N	❑ Y ❑ N
_____	_____	❑ Y ❑ N	❑ Y ❑ N
_____	_____	❑ Y ❑ N	❑ Y ❑ N
_____	_____	❑ Y ❑ N	❑ Y ❑ N
_____	_____	❑ Y ❑ N	❑ Y ❑ N
_____	_____	❑ Y ❑ N	❑ Y ❑ N
_____	_____	❑ Y ❑ N	❑ Y ❑ N

NOTIFIED BY: ❑ Phone   ❑ In Person
                   ❑ Memo   ❑ Other _____

MATERIALS NEEDED: ❑ Hand-outs   ❑ Overheads
                        ❑ Reports   ❑ Other _____

PRE-MEETING PREPARATION?   ❑ Yes   ❑ No

ATTIRE: ❑ Business   ❑ Casual   ❑ Business Casual

Adapted from *How to Manage Projects, Priorities & Deadlines: The Art of Getting It Done* audio series by Jonathan and Susan Clark. National Press Publications, Shawnee Mission, KS, 1992

Seating Arrangements

Once you've selected the room for your presentation, you need to determine the best seating arrangement. Consider the size of the room, the number of people in attendance and any special needs of your audience.

For example, if you have individuals in wheelchairs or other special-needs participants, you must make sure that the room is fully accessible. Arrange for ramps, if needed, and make sure aisles are wide enough to accommodate wheelchairs. Remove chairs from the middle of the room so that anyone in a wheelchair can sit with the group, rather than being parked at the side or back of the room.

When you select a seating arrangement, you have many more options than you might think. Here are some examples, with the advantages and disadvantages of each.

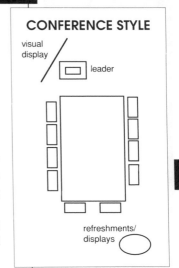

- **Conference Style:** The conference style setup usually can accommodate four to 16 people. This is a good choice for a small room and is conducive to conducting a working session. While everyone can easily see the speaker, some people may have to turn in their chairs slightly to see any visual displays. If you walk around during your presentation, you need to stay in the front of the room so that you don't walk behind members of your audience. This arrangement allows for easy interaction among participants because of the closeness of the arrangement. The speaker must be careful when using slides, transparencies or a flip chart in this setting. It's very easy to stand in someone's line of sight because of the size of the room.

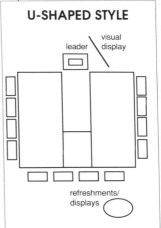

- **U-Shaped Style**: The U-shape is also appropriate to use in smaller groups of four to 16 people. Unlike the conference style, however, participants find it difficult to talk unless they are sitting beside one another. This style provides for big group interaction, but people must speak up. It's also very easy for people to table-chat with the person next to them.

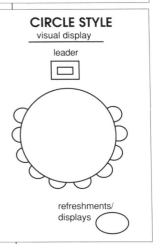

- **Circle Style**: The circle style is more suited to small groups. The leader can either stand at the front of the room or sit down with the group for a more informal presentation. A restricted view of audio/visual materials is one drawback to this seating arrangement.

5

POD STYLE

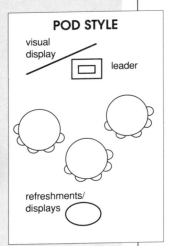

• **Pod Style**: The pod style is appropriate for a working session, as each table can work independently. This style is suited to a speaker who likes to walk among the participants. It also offers diverse work groups a way to organize and discuss agenda items.

CLASSROOM STYLE

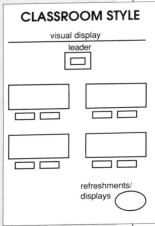

• **Classroom Style**. The classroom style is more formal than the pod style. In this arrangement, the speaker can move back and forth across the front of the room or down the aisle. This allows the speaker to get closer to all members and helps to make all participants feel a part of the group. It can be used with almost any size of group. It's important to give each person adequate table space to work. Straddling table legs gets old very quickly. Voice amplification must also be considered, because the classroom style causes people to move away from the speaker.

CHEVRON STYLE

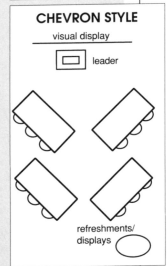

• **Chevron Style**: The chevron style is a variation of the classroom style. It can be used with both small and large groups because the angled tables enable all participants to see the speaker and the visuals.

- **Theater Style**: The theater style is the most often used set-up for large groups. Since no tables are included, this arrangement isn't a good idea if participants need to take notes. Leaving at least one aisle in the middle will allow the speaker to get closer to the participants and help to keep their attention.

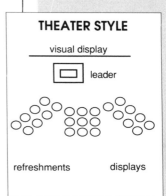

Regardless of the selected style, it is best if you are able to walk within a few feet of the audience. This allows everyone to feel a part of the presentation. This is difficult to accomplish if the speaker remains at the front of the room or hides behind a lectern.

5

SEATING ARRANGEMENT CHART

The chart below will help you determine which arrangement to use for your presentation if you have some flexibility.

Style	Room Size	Group Size
Conference	Small	Small
U-Shaped	Small/medium	Small
Circle	Small/medium	Small/medium
Pod	Medium	Medium+
Classroom	Medium	Large
Chevron	Medium+	Large
Theater	Large	Large

Logistics Checklist

Refer to this checklist after planning the logistics of your presentation. It will keep you from forgetting any of the important details.

☐ I have chosen a time that is convenient for me, as well as for the people I will address.

☐ I have ordered refreshments and/or lunch.

☐ I have scheduled the room.

☐ I have inspected the room prior to my presentation.

☐ I have arranged for the audio/visual equipment I will need. (This is discussed more completely in the next section.)

☐ I have decided to use the following room arrangement. (Be sure to give a copy of the diagram to whomever is responsible for setting up the room.)

   ☐ Conference style
   ☐ U-shaped style
   ☐ Circle style
   ☐ Pod style
   ☐ Classroom style
   ☐ Chevron style
   ☐ Theater style

FACILITIES PLANNER

Meeting Date: _____ Start Time: _____
Location: _____ End Time: _____

MATERIALS:

Qty.		Qty.		Qty.	
___	Tables	___	Slide Projector(s)	___	Easel(s)
___	Chairs	___	VCR(s)	___	Extension Cord(s)
___	Podium/lectern	___	Monitor(s)	___	Pens/Pencils
___	Microphones(s)	___	Screen(s)	___	Notepads
___	O/H Projector(s)	___	Flip-chart(s)	___	Other _____

ROOM SET-UP:

❏ Classroom ❏ Theater ❏ U-shaped ❏ Circle
❏ Conference ❏ Other _____

REFRESHMENTS:

No. People: _____

❏ Coffee/Tea/Soda Time: _____
❏ Menu Attached Time: _____
❏ Other: _____ Time: _____

Provider: _____ Time: _____
Date Ordered: _____ Phone: _____
Date Confirmed: _____

	Required?	Available? Y	N
Adjustable lighting			
Adjustable temperature			
Back-up audio/visual equipment			
Sound system			
Acceptable decor			
Comfortable seating			
ADA compliance			
Telephone(s)			
Out-of-town accommodations			
Transportation			

5

Visual Aids

"Every Picture Tells a Story, Don't It?"
Rod Stewart

The purpose of visual aids is threefold:

1. reiterate/support your verbal presentation
2. hold attention
3. serve as a "planned interruption," a monotony breaker.

Unless visual aids are carefully prepared and used appropriately, however, they can detract from your presentation, rather than add to it.

Still not convinced? Read on.

- A University of Wisconsin study noted an improvement of 200 percent when vocabulary was taught with visuals.
- Harvard University studies consistently show a 14 to 38 percent improvement in retention through the use of audio/visuals.
- In *Presentation Plus*, David Peoples states that audiences gain 75 percent of their information through seeing, 13 percent through hearing, and 12 percent through touch, taste, etc.
- A study conducted by the Wharton School of Business found that when visuals were used, people were more likely to say "Yes" and act on recommendations.

Before making a final decision about your visual aids, ask yourself these five questions:

1. Is the visual clear, obvious, readable and simple?
2. Does the visual communicate a single idea?
3. Is it relevant?
4. Is it interesting?
5. Is it accurate?

Listed below is an explanation of the various types of visual aids and when they are most appropriate for your presentations. Note the benefit and drawback of each type of audio/visual as you decide which to choose.

- **Flip charts or marker boards**: These are most effective when making an informal presentation to a small group of 15 or less. They promote discussion and encourage audience interaction. (Note: Use a flip chart instead of a marker board if you think you might have to refer to something you've written down.) You can use flip charts with the lights up and can easily refer to information to give instant feedback and reinforcement of group discussions. Three major drawbacks are that they must be legible and readable, they are difficult to transport, and are not convenient for groups larger than 20.

5

- **Videotapes**: Videotapes are often useful when making a presentation that illustrates how to do something. For example, if your presentation is on relieving stress, a videotape showing individuals doing relaxation exercises may be very effective. Don't use videos that are more than 20 to 25 minutes in length because you're liable to lose your audience's attention. Be sure to preview the video all the way through to make sure it works properly. Videos are great for professional image, can be rented for specific topics, yet are very poor for audience involvement. Videos can compensate for lack of knowledge or experience, but watching a TV is a "passive" event for many. Finally, prepare a list of specific "de-brief" questions. Showing a video without relating it to your subject matter is a sure sign of a novice presenter.

Don't use videos more than 25 minutes in length.

- **Overhead projectors**: Using overheads allows you to prepare information ahead of time and gives your presentation a more professional, polished look. They are most effective with small to medium-sized groups as long as all participants can read the text. You can use overheads you prepared in advance and add information using a grease pencil. For ease in reading, make sure your letters on the original are at least one-fourth inch high. A good policy when making transparencies is to place them on the floor. If you can read them while standing, the type is large enough. The advantages of using overhead projectors include:
  1. You can use overheads without having to dim the lights.
  2. They are easy to transport.
  3. You can rent them easily in different locations.

One drawback is that transparencies must be constructed

professionally, following certain guidelines (e.g., no more than seven words per line, seven lines per page, between 1-1/2" and 2" high, fonts no less than 30 points in size). Colors make them more persuasive and credible, with three colors maximum. Avoid red or green; they are more difficult to read.

Check your slides and projector after they have been set up.

- **35-mm slide projector**: Like overheads, slide projectors allow you to prepare your material ahead of time. They are generally set up in the middle or back of the room. Most are equipped with a remote advance/reverse control that allows you to operate the projector without standing next to it. Unlike overheads, you can't add new information to the slides after they have been prepared. Also, remember to check your slides and projector after they have been set up. It's easy to put your slides in backwards or upside-down. Slides are good for a professional appearance. One drawback is that the lights must be lowered, causing the audience to "doze."

- **Handouts and workbooks**: Handouts can be used to provide information not included in your presentation or to highlight facts that are included in your presentation. If your presentation includes training, a workbook can be used to test participants on the information you have given them or to provide them with a reference they can use later. Handouts and workbooks can be placed on the audience's chairs before the presentation or handed out before, during or after the presentation. Caution: You must be very good or your presentation will compete with the handout for your audience's attention.

Making Sure Everything Goes Right

There is nothing more exasperating for an audience and more frustrating for a speaker than to have an overhead projector that doesn't work or slides that appear on the screen upside-down or reversed. This is a sure indication of the presenter's lack of preparation and polish. To avoid this, use the following checklist whenever your presentation calls for audio/visual support materials.

Audio/Visual Checklist

☐ I checked the length of all extension cords and electrical current to the available outlets.

☐ The slide projector works and is set up properly. The lens is focused.

☐ I have a spare bulb and know how to change it.

☐ If a slide becomes stuck in the projector, I know how to remove it.

☐ I have previewed my carousel of slides for proper sequence and position. They advance without sticking.

☐ I have checked the microphone for volume and clarity.

☐ I have assigned someone to control the lights in the room and have instructed him on my needs.

☐ I have sat in various seats throughout the room to ensure that everyone can see.

☐ I have completed a brief run-through of the audio/visual portion of my presentation.

☐ I have double-checked my slides or transparencies for spelling errors or inaccurate information.

Tips for Using Audio/Visuals

Don't talk to the audio/visuals — this is one of the greatest flaws of presenters.

- Dim the lights before showing slides. Consider assigning someone to operate your lights.

- Make sure the slide or transparency being projected shows only what you are currently talking about.

- Avoid intermittent use of slides during your presentation. Arrange your speech so that all the slides are shown in an unbroken sequence, concept by concept.

- Look at the audience while the slides are being projected. No one is interested in the back of your head. Don't talk to the audio/visuals — this is one of the greatest flaws of presenters.

- When you are finished using the slides, turn the lights up immediately and then continue your presentation.

- When pointing out specific information on a transparency, DO NOT walk up to the screen and point. Place a pencil or other "pointer" on the overhead glass.

A Word of Warning About Visual Aids

Visual aids are a necessary component of professional presentations, technical briefings, administrative reporting and a host of other instructional sessions. Certain audiences expect them and judge professionalism accordingly. However, when slides are projected in a darkened room or a videotape is shown, the speaker immediately becomes isolated from the audience. There is danger of losing some of the personal contact that is essential to good presentations.

What you gain by using visual aids may be more imagined than real. Carefully weigh the advantages and disadvantages before deciding to use visual aids. The following chart can assist you in selecting the most effective visual.

VISUAL AIDS AT A GLANCE

VISUAL	GROUP SIZE	RECOMMENDATIONS
Handouts	All sizes	Mail them along with the presentation agenda; place them on seats if they're needed during the meeting or distribute them at the exit if not used during the presentation; include instructions and sources; check page sequences; color-code multiple handouts for easy reference.
Overhead transparencies	Medium to large	Use no more than seven words per line and seven lines per overhead; use letters that are one-fourth of an inch high; use one or two type styles and no more than three colors; keep an extra lamp and extension cord handy; use the "on/off" switch to break the "hypnotizing" effect of the overhead projection.
Slides	All sizes	Test for correct positioning of slides; keep display to 25 minutes or less; keep illustrations simple and clear.
Videotapes	Small to medium	Use a 25-inch or larger monitor screen; preset video in proper position and check tracking; show for 25 minutes or less; be sure to debrief.
Flip charts/marker boards	Small	Use no more than eight lines in a vertical format; use two- to four-inch letters with a two-inch leading between rows; use no more than 20 words per page; put two blank pages between each pair of prepared flips; elevate displays for larger groups; use dark markers.

5

Arrive Early

Once you've completed your initial preparation, you're ready to go, right? Just about. Don't leave anything to chance. Arrive at the site of your presentation 15 minutes to one hour early. The more familiar you are with the room and the setup, the less time you will need. Once you arrive, take the following steps:

- **Make sure the chairs, tables and all equipment have been arranged the way you requested.** Walk around the room and sit in different chairs to get an idea of what your audience will see. Ensure that movement in and out of chairs is easily made.

- **Check the temperature of the room**. If you are talking to a large group, it's OK if the room is a little cool. Once everyone arrives, the temperature will rise. If, however, it is entirely too cool or too warm, find someone who can help you adjust the thermostat.

- **Check your microphone**. Make sure the microphone works and that you know how to adjust the volume. Mentally note how far you can walk before you run out of cord, or notice feedback pockets that "squawk" with wireless microphones.

- **Check for refreshments**. If you have ordered refreshments, make sure everything is set up as requested.

- **Get yourself one or two glasses of water**. These will come in handy when giving your presentation. Take small sips during exercises or only when you really must have a drink.

- **Check the number of chairs.** Count the number of chairs and make sure there are enough. Remove extra chairs prior to the participants' arrival.

- **Check your appearance in the mirror**. Straighten your tie or comb your hair. Be sure to put on a smile!

- **Review your notes**. Go over your notes one last time.

- **Take a few deep breaths and relax, you're ready to go!**

Last-Minute Checklist

Take this checklist with you the day of your presentation. It will help ensure that the room logistics are correct.

☐ The chairs have been arranged as requested.

☐ The temperature of the room is comfortable.

☐ I know how to control the thermostat or whom to contact if it needs adjusting during my presentation.

☐ The refreshments are set up as requested.

☐ I have arranged for water to drink during my presentation.

☐ There are enough chairs.

☐ I am informed about the emergency-exit location and procedures.

☐ I know where the closest telephones are located.

☐ I have located the men's and ladies' restrooms.

Double-checking and even triple-checking everything from the room to your appearance is imperative. If everything runs smoothly, you will be more confident and your presentation will have a polished, professional look.

5

5

Questions for Personal Development

1. What is the major emphasis of this chapter?

    _____

    _____

    _____

    _____

2. What are the most important things you learned from this chapter?

    _____

    _____

    _____

    _____

3. How can you apply what you learned to your current job?

    _____

    _____

    _____

    _____

4. How will you go about making these improvements?

    _____

    _____

    _____

    _____

5. How can you monitor improvement?

    _____

    _____

    _____

    _____

6. Summarize the changes you expect to see in yourself one year from now.

    _____

    _____

    _____

Summary

It's the little things that can make or break how your audience perceives your presentation. If the visuals are unreadable or the temperature is excessive, you can bet that most participants will leave your session frustrated or confused.

Paying attention to details is a must. In this chapter you learned the importance of double- and triple-checking everything from room setup to the extension cord for your projector.

When preparing for your presentation, remember to do the following:

Arrive early and check everything — including yourself — one last time.

5

- Schedule a time and place that will be convenient for your audience.

- Arrange for refreshments if the presentation length is more than two hours.

- Select a seating arrangement that best suits your presentation.

- Use audio/visual materials effectively.

- Arrive early and check everything — including yourself — one last time.

Now that you're fully prepared, it's time to move on to the second section of the book — Delivering Your Presentation.

C HAPTER 6

Delivering Your Presentation

After you have prepared and practiced, you're ready to make your presentation. You can feel confident knowing that you have taken all the necessary steps to ensure a good presentation. If your palms moisten and your knees begin to knock, don't worry. Remember, your reaction is just butterflies and you can make them work for you rather than against you. Use the rush of adrenaline to give a truly energized presentation.

> *Use the rush of adrenaline to give a truly energized presentation!*

Qualities of a Skillful Presenter

Being a skillful presenter takes a lot more than preparation and practice. Good presenters also possess certain qualities. Do you have these qualities? Study the following list and put a check next to the ones you possess. No individual will meet all the points, but the successful presenter will make a conscious effort to continually improve her presentation skills.

QUALITIES OF A SKILLFUL PRESENTER

☐ 1. **Self-control**: Skillful presenters remain in control, regardless of what happens. They don't let internal or external forces ruin their presentation.

☐ 2. **Poise:** Not only is it important for a presenter to know her presentation content, she also must be perceived as someone who knows the subject matter about which she is speaking.

☐ 3. **Awareness of people, time and place**: A good presenter will be cognizant not only of the people attending her presentation, but also of the most convenient time and place for them. A good presenter starts her presentation on time and ends on time.

☐ 4. **Tact:** Tasteless comments or jokes are bound to hurt individuals, as well as the presentation. Tactfulness is an important trait for all presenters. If in doubt, remain silent.

☐ 5. **Decisiveness:** Allowing participants to ask questions means that the presenter must be quick on her feet, able to process the question, facilitate group responses and provide "suggested" answers.

☐ 6. **Persuasiveness**: A presenter is usually trying to get an audience to act or think in a specific way. In order to be successful, you must be persuasive.

☐ 7. **Enthusiasm**: If you can't exude true enthusiasm for the topic you are presenting, then you can't expect your audience to be enthusiastic either.

☐ 8. **Honesty and directness**: If your presentation deals with an unpopular or controversial subject, being honest and direct may be difficult. In the long run, honesty — no matter how painful — will pay off. These two attributes also affect your credibility.

☐ 9. **Flexibility:** Professional presenters should avoid being too rigid with timing issues. It is important to allow the audience's interaction to occur naturally, without presenter time constraints.

Delivering a Good Presentation

Delivering an interesting, attention-holding presentation requires more than standing in front of your audience and reciting what you've rehearsed. It requires constant coordination of content, delivery and audience interaction. Remember the following tips to make your presentation stand out.

> *"Honesty is the best image."*
> Ziggy

6

- **Speak lower and slower than normal**. When you slow down it drops the pitch of your voice and gives the impression of authority and power. Speaking slower will also allow those who are trying to take notes to do so without missing your next point.

- **Watch your tone of voice**. Remember, it's not only what you say, but how you say it. No matter how good the material is, if you speak in a demeaning, soft-spoken or preachy tone of voice, you will lose your credibility and probably your audience.

- **Deliver your presentation with confidence and humility.** No one likes to listen to an arrogant speaker. No matter how knowledgeable you are, you need to make your audience feel comfortable with you and the message you are presenting.

Tips to Help Your Presentation Run More Smoothly

Look for something that you have in common with your audience.

No matter how much you prepare or rehearse, things can still go wrong. The following tips, however, will help you keep those things to a minimum.

- **Prearrange seating**. People tend to settle down more quickly if you decide where they will sit. Additionally, this technique gives you an opportunity to separate people who have a tendency to carry on their own conversations. This works best when you have a position of authority over your audience; otherwise, they may "overrule" your arrangement.

- **Assign a scribe**. If you are leading a discussion and want to highlight the most important points on an easel, ask a member of the audience to write down the information for you. If you want to send out follow-up reports, ask someone to take notes and type them up for distribution.

- **Be a wise timekeeper**. Remove your watch before you start speaking, and place it where you can easily read it. This will remind you to stay on schedule without distracting your audience. Some speakers find it helpful to let someone signal at key times to help stay on schedule.

- **Follow your agenda**. Everyone in the audience should have a copy of your agenda. To keep the meeting flowing smoothly, follow this agenda and don't allow people to steer you off course. If others will be participating in the presentation, make sure their names and topics are on the agenda, too. Be sure to leave time for questions and answers.

- **Look for common denominators**. When possible, look for something that you have in common with your audience and use it to build rapport. For example, if you know that members of your audience are interested in professional basketball you might say, "That sure was a good game last night. Those are two teams I'm sure we will see in the playoffs." This is done as a transition and is planned.

- **If you don't know an answer, say so.** Tell the person you will get back to her — and follow through. Or, ask someone in the audience to research the answer for you. For example, "That's a good question, Jim. I'm not exactly sure what our budget is for next year. Betty, would you please look that up and let Jim know after the meeting?"

- **Don't be afraid to use your audience's resources.** No one knows all the answers. If someone asks you a question and you don't know the answer, say, "Excellent question, Mary. That's something I hadn't considered. What does everyone else think about that idea?" This is also an excellent way to let experienced, knowledgeable participants share their "expertise" and avoid boredom.

- **Color-code your notes to make them easier to follow.** Use yellow to indicate that it's time to put up an overhead or use orange to indicate that you need to take a break. This method helps you know at a glance what you should do next. You also may want to use another color, maybe blue, to indicate optional material. By doing this, if your presentation is running long, you simply can delete the blue material.

- **Number the pages of your notes.** In the event that you accidentally drop your notes, this tip can be a lifesaver. The best way to keep control in your presentation is to plan for errors.

- **Place overhead transparencies in clear sheet protectors** and number them sequentially; if using a lengthy workbook or handout, number your overheads to match the workbook page.

- **Store overhead transparencies in a three-ring binder.** While speaking, take them from the binder to the overhead projector and then re-insert them in the binder. They will be ready to use and will stay in the proper order.

Don't be afraid to use your audience's resources.

6

Checklist

To ensure that your presentation goes smoothly, use the following checklist before you begin.

☐ I have prearranged seating and have placed table tents or name cards at each chair.

☐ I have assigned scribes.

(Name) _____ will write important points on the easel.

(Name) _____ will take notes and send out a follow-up report by (date) _____.

☐ I have planned my presentation so I can stick to my agenda.

☐ I have thought about common denominators. The thing I have in common with this audience or the thing I know these audience members have in common with each other is (topic) _____.

_____

☐ I have color-coded my notes.

☐ I have numbered the pages of my notes.

☐ I have triple-checked the equipment.

Now that you've completed all these steps, it's time to give a great presentation!

Questions for Personal Development

1. What is the major emphasis of this chapter?

    _____
    _____
    _____
    _____

2. What are the most important things you learned from this chapter?

    _____
    _____
    _____
    _____

3. How can you apply what you learned to your current job?

    _____
    _____
    _____
    _____

4. How will you go about making these improvements?

    _____
    _____
    _____
    _____

5. How can you monitor improvement?

    _____
    _____
    _____
    _____

6. Summarize the changes you expect to see in yourself one year from now.

    _____
    _____
    _____
    _____

6

Summary

Avoid negative body language.

For many people, actually delivering their presentation is the most difficult part of speaking. If you've prepared and practiced adequately, you have nothing to worry about.

When delivering your presentation, remember these tips:

- Speak lower and slower than normal to give the impression of authority and power.

- Avoid using preachy or demeaning tones.

- Be careful that you don't come across as arrogant.

- Your actions speak louder than words. Avoid negative body language, such as slouches, hands in pockets, lowered head and shoulders, pacing.

- Prearrange seating to help your audience get settled more quickly.

- Assign a scribe and timekeeper.

- Follow your agenda.

- Look for common interests with the audience.

- If you don't know the answer, say so.

- Ask members of the audience for their input.

- Color-code your notes.

- Triple-check your equipment.

CHAPTER 7

Thinking on Your Feet

The success of your presentation depends not only on how well you make your presentation but on how your audience perceives you. This chapter will provide you with tips for increasing your credibility by using humor, handling interruptions and dealing with rude or hostile people.

> *It's important that your audience believes you and trusts you.*

Increasing Your Credibility

As a presenter, it's important that your audience believes you and trusts you. But, how believable and trustworthy you are actually depends on how your audience perceives you. If people don't view you as believable and trustworthy, they will have problems accepting what you are trying to tell them.

Here are some questions to help you think about how to increase your credibility with your audience. Note any areas where you feel you need some work.

AM I CREDIBLE?

		Yes	No
1.	I contact the group or a liaison before preparation to learn specifics that are applicable to the presentation.	[ ]	[ ]
2.	I have references about the group added to my speech.	[ ]	[ ]
3.	I plan for and use their own industry and/or business jargon.	[ ]	[ ]
4.	I regularly refer to specifics about their business situations.	[ ]	[ ]
5.	I start my presentations on time.	[ ]	[ ]
6.	I'm well prepared.	[ ]	[ ]
7.	When I am asked a question, I make my answer short and direct. I avoid getting sidetracked.	[ ]	[ ]
8.	I use visual aids to get my point across.	[ ]	[ ]
9.	I not only tell but show my audience what to do.	[ ]	[ ]
10.	I give specific examples.	[ ]	[ ]
11.	I make certain everyone understands what I have just said before moving on to another topic.	[ ]	[ ]
12.	I keep my presentation under control and well-focused.	[ ]	[ ]
13.	I address hostility instead of ignoring it.	[ ]	[ ]
14.	I summarize periodically to highlight significant points.	[ ]	[ ]
15.	I establish a clear timeline and end my presentations on time.	[ ]	[ ]
16.	Before my audience arrives, members have received a copy of my agenda.	[ ]	[ ]
17.	When possible, I call audience members by name.	[ ]	[ ]
18.	I don't hide behind a lectern, but instead walk around the room to have closer contact with the audience.	[ ]	[ ]

Using Humor

When used appropriately, humor can add spice and interest to your presentation. It builds rapport, anchors information, illustrates a "how to" and makes a point. If it is used inappropriately, however, it can doom an otherwise good presentation to failure.

Following are some tips for using humor in your presentations.

- **Use humor that suits you**. Humor should be natural, not forced. If you force humor, your audience will tune you out. Rather than copying another's style or going to a book and lifting a joke, find a style you are comfortable with that can breathe life and interest into the presentation.

- **Use humor as a mental recess**. If you're presenting a particularly heavy or serious topic and you notice your audience is starting to wear down, interject some humor. It will help lighten things up and bring your audience back to attention. Mark Twain has a multitude of quotes that can be appropriate in many situations. For example, if you find you've written a word incorrectly, you could refer to Twain: "Pity the man who can spell a word only one way."

- **Use humor as a bridge or transition**. Humor can be used to make a transition from one topic to another. For example, if you are getting ready to talk about stress you might say, "No one here has ever had a bad day, right? That brings us to our next topic — stress." Or, "Did you know that stressed is desserts spelled backward?"

- **Don't tell inappropriate jokes**. There is nothing that can make a presentation bomb quicker than an inappropriate joke that insults one or more members of your audience. Avoid jokes about women, men, religion, politics, ethnic backgrounds or other topics your audience might find offensive. A good guideline is: If you're not sure whether the joke will offend someone, don't tell it! Some of the safest and best jokes you can tell are on yourself.

> *"Everything is funny as long as it is happening to somebody else."*
> Will Rogers

7

Interruptions

"When nothing is sure, everything is possible."
Margaret Drabble

Interruptions, whether they are from your audience or from external sources, can be very disruptive to your presentation. To limit interruptions from your audience, let people know the guidelines up front. For example, say, "I'm going to talk for about 10 minutes. After that I will answer any questions you may have." If, on the other hand, you want to address questions as they arise, make that clear, too. For example, "If you have any questions about what we're talking about, please raise your hand and I'll address them right away."

If you have made it clear that you will take questions at the end of your presentation and someone still interrupts, simply say, "Excellent question, Bill. We will deal with that in just a few minutes. Hold that question and you will be the first one up during the question and answer period." By doing this, you address Bill, yet remind him and the rest of the audience that the time for questions is after your presentation.

If possible, discuss interruptions from external sources in advance. For example, if you know there will be a meeting in the room next door and you suspect it could get loud, inform your audience early. Say, "There is another meeting going on next door. If the noise bothers you, let me know and I'll close the door."

It's also important to address emergencies and how messages will be handled should interruptions arise. Will you answer a ringing phone? Will you wait for someone to return? Is a message board available?

Another significant interruption in today's electronic age is the "beeper." How will you handle beepers? One suggestion used by many corporations during business meetings is to have every participant "check" his beeper with a secretary who can monitor, respond and screen many interruptions.

With preparation and practice, you can be ready for any type of interruption.

Interruptions During the Presentation:
There are four options when you are challenged with interruptions:
1. You can ignore them. Remember, it's your presentation and people are addressed at your discretion. By simply ignoring the interruption, you risk losing credibility but may save embarrassment. Watch any presidential briefing

for an excellent example of ignoring some interruptions and addressing others.

2. You can discourage them through body language (frown, lack of eye contact, etc.). Once you make eye contact with an interrupter, you must either respond or be seen as rude.

3. You can address the interruption. You can make direct eye contact, answer the question and then restate the interruption rules you established at the beginning of your talk.

   Another effective technique is to stand next to the interrupter and answer the question, talking to the group. Once finished, move away from the interrupter without making further eye contact. You also may have a habitual interrupter. A statement like, "These have been some interesting questions. Before we go on let's make it possible for everyone to participate."

   One presenter hands out three M&Ms to everyone at the beginning of the briefing. Participants must eat an M&M every time they interrupt. When the M&Ms are gone, so are the opportunities to interrupt.

4. You can use assertive statements.
   - Setting limits — Example: "I will handle three questions." Or, "I will answer your issues during break."
   - Fogging — Example: "I can see there are some interested people with lots of excellent comments."
   - Dominance — Call a break and talk to individuals.

5. You can "put the person off." Simply say, "That's a great question; I think I'll cover that later. Let's talk after the presentation if I miss it."

> *"Problems are only opportunities in work clothes."*
> Henry Kaiser

7

Dealing with Rude People

Hopefully, you won't encounter many rude people when making presentations. These individuals shout out things like, "yeah, right," laugh, yawn loudly or try other methods to distract you and members of your audience. If you have rude people in your audience, use the following alternatives to deal with them.

- **Ignore the interruption**. Pay no attention to the individual. Continue talking, regardless of your annoyance. Many times these people are simply looking for attention. If you don't give it to them, they eventually will stop. If it is a large group, you need to stop until the interruption dies down. A high percentage of your audience will sympathize with you and try to help you. If you create a contest or "show up" the rude person, the audience will polarize.

- **Address the interruption.** Stop your presentation, look at the individual and say, "Linda, is there a problem?" Sometimes putting people on the spot will catch them off guard, causing them to discontinue their behavior. That's not always the case. Realize that if you choose this approach, you basically have lost control of the situation because you've turned the floor over to the heckler. It's also important to hear the interruption. By separating the interrupter from the interruption, you may be able to talk about an important issue, while controlling the rude person.

- **Be assertive**. Address the individual but don't invite him to respond. For example, say, "Jerry, I want to hear what you have to say, but please wait until I am finished." This approach may put a temporary end to the interruption.

- **Offer to clarify what you are saying**. This works well if you have two or more individuals who are talking among themselves. For example, say, "Bill and Pete, I know you are probably discussing something I haven't explained yet. Is there something I can clarify for you?" This will get their attention again.

- **Give the individual a knowing look**. If mobile, walk in the individual's general vicinity and then back away while looking directly at him. This action may cause the person to stop his offensive behavior.

- **Use humor**. If you are addressing peers or members of your team and two or more of them are carrying on a conversation, try humor. For example, say with a smile, "Sue and Betty, am I going to have to separate you?"

Give the individual a knowing look.

7

- **Use silence.** Oftentimes, pausing until the interruption is complete will create such an uncomfortable silence that the offender will stop.

If nothing you do works, leave the individual or individuals alone until after the meeting. Then approach them and say, "I think it was unfair of you not to give me your attention. You made it difficult for those who wanted to hear what I had to say." By doing this, you let them know that you were aware of their rudeness. They also know that if they try it again, you won't tolerate it.

The most important thing in dealing with rude people is to stay in control. Don't let them know you are upset. Remember: ANGER is only one letter away from DANGER.

Behavior not confronted will in all likelihood continue. You must remember the time and energy invested warrants a fair hearing. Rude participants make that impossible. Care enough about your content, your time and your investment to confront counter-productive behavior.

> *"Tension blocks the flow of thought power."*
> Norman Vincent Peale

Dealing with Hostile People

If people are hostile during your presentation, they either don't want to hear what you have to say or they don't want to be there. If you know that a particular individual will be hostile or negative, talk with him before your presentation and excuse him if possible.

Addressing the issue as soon as possible will help you gain control of the situation. Approach the person and say, "I know you will have some problems with what I am about to say, so let's sit down now and talk about your concerns." By doing this, you defuse the situation and may even gain a supporter.

If the entire group is hostile, try winning the members over one step at a time by using indisputable facts or logic. Acknowledge the emotion before you deal with the issue. By doing this, your audience will relax and prepare to listen to you. For example, say, "I know that most of you don't like the fact that this company is merging with another, but that is indeed what is happening. What I want to do today is tell you what this merger will mean to this department and each of you." Ignoring the emotion will be detrimental to your presentation.

7

Case Studies

Examine the following case studies that deal with managing rude and hostile people. What could the presenter have done to diffuse the situation? Check your responses with those listed at the bottom of the page.

Case Study Number One: Marge has been asked to explain to everyone in the office how to use the new office copier. She asks five people at a time to come into the copier room for her presentation. When Marge approaches Rob, he snaps at her and says, "I don't know why you want me to learn this. I'm a manager. I shouldn't have to make my own copies." Marge informs him that *everyone* has to learn how to use the machine and proceeds to the copy room. Marge has carefully prepared her presentation and takes the group through all the steps demonstrating how to make copies and use all the special features of the machine. At the end of her presentation, Rob steps forward and says, "I don't know why you're telling us this. All I want to know is how to make one copy!"

C A S E

S T U D Y

Solution: Upon sensing his aggression, Marge could have said, "Rob, you're right. You can probably find someone else to show you how to make copies. However, these people are interested in learning about all of the copier's features. If you're interested, feel free to stay with us."

Case Study Number Two: Bob is giving a presentation on the company's new health plan. Many employees are unhappy with the change. About five minutes into his presentation, Bob notices two employees in the back of the room talking to each other. He begins to talk louder and louder. Suddenly he stops, and yells, "Would you guys shut up and listen?"

C

A

S

E

7

S

T

U

D

Y

Solution: Rather than yelling at the talkers, a better method for stopping the interruption would be to simply stop speaking. The silence from you and the audience would amplify the two interrupters' conversation, causing embarrassment. Proceed when they have returned their attention to you.

Case Study Number Three: Tim is making a presentation to a group of salespeople about a new product. He tells the audience that he will address questions at the end of his presentation.   About five minutes into his remarks, a member of the audience blurts out, "Do you really think we can sell that thing?" Tim stops his presentation and snaps, "Yes, I think you can sell this thing. If you just give me a minute, I'll tell you how!"

C
A
S
E

S
T
U
D
Y

7

Solution: Address the interrupter by saying, "That's an interesting question. I'd be happy to open up the floor for discussion at the end of the program." This should send a clear message that you will not tolerate outbursts of this kind.

Case Study Number Four: Larry is explaining the company's impending layoffs and associated severance package to a group of employees. He begins his presentation by saying, "As you all know, over the next year many of you will lose your jobs. Today I am going to explain to you the company's severance package." Members of the audience begin to mumble, but Larry keeps right on talking as if nothing is happening.

C
A
S
E

S
T
U
D
Y

7

Solution: Because Larry is prepared for the audience's negative reaction, he should begin the presentation with a group exercise or discussion that allows the participants to vent their feelings. At the end of the exercise, he can summarize their comments and transition into his presentation. Failing to address their concerns initially will prohibit his audience from focusing on his information.

Exercise

Now that you've looked at some case studies, think of a time when you made a presentation and you were faced with a rude or hostile person. What did you do? What could you have done to be more effective?

Situation Involving Rudeness/Hostility	What I Did	What I Could Have Done

If Someone Falls Asleep

No matter how compelling your presentation, occasionally someone will fall asleep or begin to doze. If this happens to you, simply increase your volume and walk toward the individual. Don't look directly at him, but stay in the vicinity for a few minutes. By doing this, you will hopefully recapture the dozer's attention without needlessly embarrassing him.

Additional strategies include:
1. Putting your hand on shoulders
2. Calling a break
3. Simply ignoring the person sleeping

If you've done your best to prepare and have truly designed your talk to impact your audience, then the "dozer" obviously needs sleep more than he needs information. Relax, don't take it personally, and remember there's still a room of people who need and want to hear what you have to say. Talk to them.

> *"What is this, an audience or an oil painting?"*
> Milton Berle

7

129

Questions for Personal Development

1. What is the major emphasis of this chapter?

    _____
    _____
    _____
    _____

2. What are the most important things you learned from this chapter?

    _____
    _____
    _____
    _____

3. How can you apply what you learned to your current job?

    _____
    _____
    _____
    _____

4. How will you go about making these improvements?

    _____
    _____
    _____
    _____

5. How can you monitor improvement?

    _____
    _____
    _____
    _____

6. Summarize the changes you expect to see in yourself one year from now.

    _____
    _____
    _____

Summary

When making a presentation, how your audience perceives you is just as important as what you have to say. What you say, how you look and how you relate to your audience members all influence their perception of you.

The following will ensure that your audience perceives you in a positive way:

"I always tried to turn every disaster into an opportunity."
John D. Rockefeller

- Build credibility with your audience.

- Use humor to add spice and interest to your presentation.

- Limit interruptions by letting your audience know the guidelines up front.

- Handle rude people tactfully, yet assertively.

- Make every effort to deal with potentially hostile people before your presentation even begins.

7

7

*C*HAPTER 8

Capturing and Maintaining Attention

In order to make an effective presentation, you must be prepared to capture your audience's attention and then maintain it. This can be done by building rapport with your audience, helping to shut out external noises, making the subject matter relevant and using your voice effectively.

Building Rapport

Building rapport with your audience is critical. If you develop rapport at the beginning of your presentation, your audience participants will sense that you have a genuine interest in them and will respond positively to what you tell them.

The following tips will help you build rapport with your audience from the start of your presentation.

- **Ask relevant questions**. Ask information-gathering questions and then assure your audience that you will answer any questions that might come up. For example, "How many of you have questions about the merger? (Pause for show of hands.) That's understandable; I did, too, before it was explained to me. Hopefully, today I can answer any questions you may have."

- **Share an exchange of needs**. The audience needs something from you and you need something from your

Be prepared to capture your audience's attention and then maintain it.

One kind word can warm three winter months.
Japanese proverb

audience members. They need information and, as a speaker, you need their approval. A good way to elicit their approval is to say things or ask questions that will evoke a response. For example, say, "When I first heard about the merger, I was a little nervous. Does anyone else feel that way?" Chances are, you will see nodding heads and maybe even some smiles. As a speaker, this tells you that you have captured their attention and they are ready to listen. These positive nods and smiles build an unspoken, but powerful, communication bridge. You'll return to those friendly eyes many times during your presentation, validating your information.

- **Watch out for *me*.** People like to talk about themselves, and, similarly, they like to hear about themselves. When making a presentation, especially one that involves showing your team how to do something, avoid using the word *I* and focus on the word *you*. For example, don't say, "This is the way *I* have done this job." Instead, say, "You will find this job easiest to do if you . . ." Tip: Always focus on "MMFI" — Make Me Feel Important.

- **Be sincere**. A genuine compliment to an audience does wonders. For example, say, "Our team has done an outstanding job this past year. Today I want to talk to you about our sales goals for the coming year."

Good presenters not only present an issue, they also present themselves. Building rapport with your audience will help ensure that your presentation runs smoothly from the start.

Rapport Worksheet

Before your next presentation, take a moment to determine what you can do to help build rapport with your audience based on the ideas outlined in this chapter.

I will involve the audience by asking these questions: _____

_____

_____

Common needs I share with my audience include: _____

_____

_____

What can I say that will engage my audience? _____

_____

_____

To evoke a response from my audience I will _____

_____

_____

A genuine compliment I can give this audience is _____

_____

_____

8

Shutting Off the External Noise

Get your audience involved immediately.

When your audience first walks into the room, every individual is thinking about something. It may be a fight with a spouse earlier that morning, a health problem or a report that is sitting on the desk waiting to be done. Your audience also brings expectations about the presentation and results to be gained from investing time in the presentation. These distractions are referred to as "external noise" or hidden agendas. Whatever the external noise, your challenge as a presenter is to turn off that noise and get your audience focused on what you are about to say. Building rapport can turn OFF the external noise.

Here are some rapport-building tips you can use to help your audience eliminate external noises.

1. **Mingle.** Before the presentation, mingle. Smile, introduce yourself, etc. This is your number one defense. Meet as many people as possible. Friends created before you speak tend to remain friends.

2. **Put something on the audience's chairs**. This could be an outline of your talk, something they can take with them or maybe an item that directly relates to your presentation. For example, if you're going to make a presentation on a product your company is releasing, you might leave one on each chair and start your presentation by asking everyone to try it.

3. **Get your audience involved immediately**. Start out your presentation by asking for involvement. For example, if you are going to give a presentation on the company's dress code, you might ask participants to pair up and tell each other if they conform to the company's dress code.

4. **Use a short, upbeat slide presentation with music or a dynamic video**. For example, if you are giving a presentation on the company's new marketing campaign, start your presentation by showing some of the company's new television commercials.

5. **Use an impressive testimonial**. This could be a letter from a satisfied customer that you read or a personal testimonial from someone else. For example, if you are making a presentation on the various benefits your company offers, you might have an individual who has used the company's educational-assistance program talk about how she was able to get a college degree through the program and, thus, was promoted in the organization.

Worksheet

Before your next presentation, think about what you can do to turn off your audience's external noises. Write down several ideas below.

1. Potential external noises include: _____

   _____

   _____

   _____

   _____

2. Tactics I can use to silence the external noise: _____

   _____

   _____

   _____

   _____

8

Maintaining Their Attention

Once you've captured your audience's attention, your next challenge is to maintain it. Typically, adults have short attention spans that shift constantly. The average person thinks at a rate of 800 words per minute, but the average person speaks at a rate of only 125 to 150 words per minute. As a result, the minds of most adults tend to wander, especially during a lengthy presentation.

Here are some tips to help you hold your audience's attention.

1. **Base your activities on the 8 to 11 Rule**. Your audience's maximum sustained attention span is eight minutes. So every eight to 11 minutes, shift activities. Move from one side of the room to the other or stop talking and ask for questions or comments. Ask the audience to write something down, or turn a page, or stop and think. Any type of change will bring their attention back to you.

2. **Follow the Rule of :20**. If you're addressing your audience for longer than 20 minutes, introduce a content change every 20 minutes. Changing topics will recapture the audience's attention. Provide an exercise or summarize the information every 20 minutes.

3. **Show intensity in your presentation**. Showing intensity can capture attention and keep it. The best way to show intensity is through your voice and your facial expressions. Raise or lower your voice; whisper perhaps. Stare at the audience individual by individual. Emphasize key words. Change your rate of speech.

   You also can add intensity through *what* you say. Telling stories or relating specific examples of what you're talking about is a great way to add intensity to your speech.

   But always keep your perspective. Any technique, story, example or other intensity-modifier should provide a brief, but powerful, interlude in your presentation. Don't fall in love with a tool and detract from your expertise.

"The opportunities will go to the men and women who have enthusiasm."
Charles F. Kettering

8

4. **Use appropriate eye contact and facial expressions**. When watching a presentation, audiences focus on the presenter's eyes and face. Making eye contact with members of the audience will make them feel as if you are talking directly to them. Use facial expressions appropriately to express emotions like surprise, sadness and disappointment.

    The old rule of looking above the heads of your audience won't work! It's your eye contact that sustains your audience's attention.

The old rule of looking above the heads of your audience won't work!

5. **Keep moving**. Movement is another way to capture attention and hold it. But beware, too much movement may overwhelm them or turn them off. Be attentive to each side of a room. If you stand to the left, shift to the right. Plan times. You could mark the floor with tape to cue in on a particular position.

    Many speakers mark four "outstanding points": one out front, one in the center and one to each side of the room. Move to the front mark when taking and asking questions, and shift from center to the sides, keeping to the center about 60 percent of the time.

Here are a few specific things you can do to capture attention:

*   Use your arms to convey enthusiasm.

*   Walk around the room to bring people back into the conversation.

*   Move toward your audience to encourage participation.

8

Using Your Voice Effectively

Crisp, polished speech patterns are another effective technique for maintaining audience attention. Also, varying the rate of your speech prevents your presentation from sounding boring. However, the professional speaker knows the necessity of warming up one's voice prior to speaking.

Try the following exercises to loosen up neck, jaw and facial muscles:

Do deep-breathing exercises.

1. **Stretch your neck**. Drop your head down as far as possible. Next, point your chin towards the ceiling.

2. **Yawn**. Simple yawning is another good way to loosen up the vocal cords. When you yawn, you tend to let the air out very slowly. This helps get the vocal cords ready to go.

3. **Do deep-breathing exercises**. Take a deep breath from your abdomen and then let it out slowly. This not only loosens your vocal cords, but also will help you relax if you're nervous about your presentation.

4. **Wag your tongue**. This will help loosen your jaw and help you to keep from tripping over words.

5. **Do voice exercises**. Doing voice exercises on a regular basis can help strengthen your voice. Or you can do them right before a presentation as a warm-up. Here are two exercises that will help strengthen your vocal cords:

   • Take a deep breath and say, "ahhh .....," holding the sound for as long as you can. This exercise gives your voice punch and increases projection. This is an excellent exercise for speakers who are soft-spoken.

   • Take a deep breath and say, "uhhh ....." in as low a tone as you can, holding the sound for as long as you can. This exercise gives your voice resonance. This is a good exercise to do if you want to lower your voice and make it more commanding.

Avoiding Problems with Your Voice

If you have to make presentations on a regular basis, you may find that by the end of the presentation you are hoarse, your mouth is dry or your voice is cracking. The following tricks of the trade will help you maintain a clear voice throughout any presentation.

• **Avoid cold liquids or drinks with caffeine**. Both ice-cold liquids and caffeine will make your vocal cords contract, causing your voice to become hoarse. Pour water ahead of time but don't drink it until it reaches room temperature. Drink water often to keep vocal cords lubricated.

• **Avoid mints or foods with sugar**. Often, speakers think that sucking on a mint or a piece of hard candy will keep their throats clear. In many cases, however, candy has just the opposite effect. Over-the-counter glycerine lozenges are preferable.

Caution: Select your times very carefully and courteously when you take a drink or place a lozenge in your mouth. It looks best to drink water while the audience is doing an exercise.

> *Avoid cold liquids or drinks with caffeine.*

8

Using Vocal Variety

Vocal variety will emphasize certain words to convey meaning and emotions so that those words "jump out" at your audience. This is the vocal equivalent of using a colorful gesture or an exclamation mark. Here are some tips for using your voice effectively.

• **Rate**: Make sure your rate is not too fast or too slow. Speed up and slow down to make certain points or recapture attention.

• **Pitch**: Change your pitch, usually moving upward on an important word or syllable. For example, "Yours is a *critical* job." To ensure that you are changing pitch effectively, practice giving your presentation on a tape recorder. Do the words you want to stand out *really* stand out?

- **Volume**: Speak louder to emphasize important words or a phrase. Speak more softly to make a point. Speaking softly is effective if you want to comfort someone, involve someone in the discussion or project gentle strength. Be careful, however, because a soft-spoken manner may label you as too meek or mild if used frequently.

- **Pause:** A pause can be an effective tool when you want to make a point. A short or even an extended pause can draw attention to a particular point. It also gives your audience extra time to think about what you've just said. It is often helpful to cue pauses in your notes.

- **Lengthening a word**: Lengthening a word can add drama. For example, you don't *neeeed* to do it that way.

As always, if you use any of these methods too often they will lose their effectiveness. But when used to provide variety, they will lend impact to your presentations.

> *A pause can be an effective tool when you want to make a point.*

Making It Relevant

If the material you are presenting isn't relevant to members of your audience, all of the attention-grabbing techniques in the world won't help. Keep asking yourself, "What's in this for them?"

Test your content by checking your frame (see Chapter 4 on Framing). Are each of the sides present? Is the benefit or application clear? Have you transitioned for a key topic of interest? Did you hook their emotions? Ask yourself with regard to every point: 1) So what? and 2) Who cares?

It may be obvious to you that your material is relevant, but have you done a good job of conveying that fact to your audience? Make sure members understand why your presentation is important to them.

For example, if you are making a presentation on the company's new computer system, structure your presentation around how the new system will benefit your audience. When speaking to the accounting department, explain how the computer will help streamline current accounting procedures. When presenting to the communications department, concentrate on the computer's design capabilities, built-in thesaurus and spell-check functions.

Other Tips for Maintaining Attention

There are several other ways to keep your audience listening.

• **Learn how to ask questions**. Even though you are the one making the presentation, you should ask questions, too. Here are some instances when your questions can be very effective.

   To ascertain if your audience is interested: "Are any of you interested in trying to use the new computer in a demonstration?"

   To capture your audience's attention: "How many of you have achieved your quota for the month?"

   To clarify a point: "Are you asking me if the new benefits package includes dental insurance?"

   To ensure understanding: "Does everyone understand exactly what holidays you will have off?"

• **Use sure-fire conversation starters or hooks to initially control or recover your audience's attention**. Here are examples of some you might use.

   — If someone gave you a million dollars, what would you do with it?

   — If you could do any type of work you wanted, what would it be?

   — If someone were to write an epitaph on your gravestone, what would it say?

   — What would you like to achieve in the next five years?

   — Whom do you most admire?

8

Things That Turn Audiences Off

As a presenter there are some tactics that you will want to avoid using. Following are some things you can do to avoid turning off your audience.

- **Avoid using clichés**. Everyone knows clichés. For example, if you say, "The grass is always greener on the other side of the fence," people will tune you out because they will have completed the phrase in their heads long before you have finished saying it.

- **Don't sermonize**. Being morally instructive is the same thing as saying, "I'm good, you're not." This is a real turn-off. Few speakers succeed with "shoulds" or "guilt trips."

- **Don't push too hard**. It's OK to push your audience a little, but avoid pushing too hard. If you push too hard, people will shut you out. They'll accomplish even less than you expected. For example, don't try to cram four hours' worth of information into three.

- **Be yourself**. Don't be phony. You are not your boss or the newscaster that you admire on television. The best style is your own style. Find it and use it consistently. When you aren't sure of your style, speak as if it were you and one other person. Style emerges from an authentic desire to "give away" what you know.

Avoid using clichés.

Planning for Attention Span

No matter how interesting your topic, you can't expect audience participants to sit on the edge of their seats throughout your entire presentation. Mentally, your audience will float in and out, catching points of relevance and then structuring what they hear into useful applications. The more effective the speaker, the less frequently the audience will mentally "check out."

Take a few moments and study the following charts on attention spans. Each is divided into three sections — an Introduction, which tends to be 10 to 15 percent of the total presentation; the Body, or 70 percent of the presentation; and the Close, which is 5 to 10 percent of the total presentation.

Following is a description of each type.

• **Instructional**: This chart shows the kind of attention span for which you want to plan when presenting basic training or instructional material. This presentation normally lasts less than two hours. You ease into the topic, capture your audience's attention at the top of the curve and then let go with a review or summary.

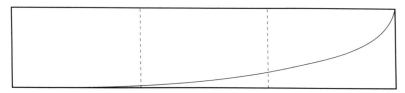

• **Motivational:** This chart illustrates the type of attention span for which you want to plan if you are presenting a motivational program, such as a sales presentation. You start out slowly, gradually build and then give your audience the most important material at the end so members leave feeling enthusiastic.

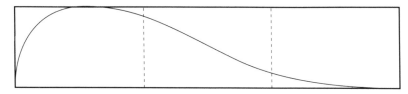

• **Keynote or Team Teaching**. If you ask another speaker to keynote your presentation, such as your boss, you will want to plan for the attention span shown in this chart. Your keynote speaker should immediately catch your audience's attention at the beginning of the session. In this instance, plan for high energy at the start, then gradually relax toward the end. Prepare the audience for a transfer. For relaxation, some presenters use jokes or stories.

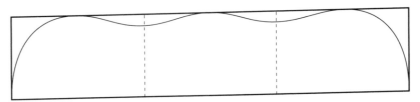

- **Drift**. Any presentation that lasts more than two hours should include an energy level that has ebbs and flows. This will help the audience maintain attention. Frame your ideas every 20 minutes. You can use exercises, stories or activities to bring the energy level up and then let it drift back down again.

If you are presenting technical or complex information, make sure that you allow your audience's attention to drift every eight to 11 minutes. Ease out with a review or summation.

Timing and Attention Span

Frame your ideas every 20 minutes.

The mind cannot absorb what the seat cannot endure! It's nearly impossible to sustain involvement beyond 90 minutes without a break. The later your presentation is given in the day, the more frequent your breaks must be. Generally an afternoon meeting should not run longer than 75 minutes without a break.

Consider what you can do to increase your team's attention when members are more than likely thinking, "When do we eat?" Specific "how to's" include:

1. Transition carefully, with an upbeat message. You might overview what you are going to say.
2. Focus on WIIFM — and tell them. Make it worth their while to stay with you.
3. Hook their attention with a great story or analogy.
4. Have some dynamite solutions that they can immediately implement or a dilemma that stretches their thinking.
5. Precall the awkward timing. Let them know you're aware of the time, and the audience will not have to wonder if you know it.

Hook their attention with a great story or analogy.

For your presentation to be truly successful, you need to capture and then maintain your audience's attention. Using the information you learned in this chapter, you can plan for your audience's attention span and keep their attention focused on what you are telling them throughout your presentation.

8

C A S E

S T U D Y

8

Case Studies

Read the following case studies and decide which attention span method would work best.

Case Study Number One. Sales have been lagging. Sue has been asked to give a presentation to the sales staff on effective selling techniques.

WHICH attention flow span should she use?

WHY?

Case Study Number Two. Tom is giving a presentation to an environmental group about his company's program to protect the environment.

WHICH attention flow span should he use?

WHY?

Case Study Number Three. Carol is conducting an orientation for new employees. She has invited the president of the company to address the group at the beginning of her presentation.

WHICH attention flow span should she use?

WHY?

1. motivational
2. instructional
3. keynote

Questions for Personal Development

1. What is the major emphasis of this chapter?

    _____
    _____
    _____
    _____

2. What are the most important things you learned from this chapter?

    _____
    _____
    _____
    _____

3. How can you apply what you learned to your current job?

    _____
    _____
    _____
    _____

4. How will you go about making these improvements?

    _____
    _____
    _____
    _____

5. How can you monitor improvement?

    _____
    _____
    _____
    _____

6. Summarize the changes you expect to see in yourself one year from now.

    _____
    _____
    _____
    _____

8

Summary

Building rapport with your audience up front and helping them shut out external noises will help you capture your audience's attention. Once you've captured their attention you need to keep it.

When giving presentations, take into account the attention-span needs of your audience and plan accordingly. You can capture and maintain your audience's attention by:

Change the pitch of your voice for emphasis.

- Making your presentation relevant.

- Using your voice effectively.

- Developing your thoughts on interesting topics.

- Avoiding conversation killers.

- Learning how to ask questions.

- Using sure-fire conversation starters or hooks.

Using vocal variety will also help to maintain your audience's attention. Follow these suggestions:

- Vary the rate and volume of your speech.

- Change the pitch of your voice for emphasis.

- Pause to make a point.

- Lengthen a word for effect.

C HAPTER 9

Bringing Your Presentation to a Close

Once you've delivered the content, the hard part is over. Now you must concentrate on the closing, the follow-through and the follow-up. In this chapter you will learn how to close a presentation and begin preparing for the next.

The close is thought to be the most important part of a presentation. It is the close that will be recalled, and it's the close that stirs your audience to action.

In the close you can recap the high points, review the critical issues, and hook them to the audience's memory through a story or parable, a quote or analogy.

Many presenters write their close first. They identify their theme, write the close, then plan the introduction so that it will support the close. The content, involvement techniques and audience tailoring all are subordinate to the close.

Most of all, you want your audience to leave with a clear understanding of the information you provided, with renewed enthusiasm and a commitment to do something with what they have learned.

> *The close is thought to be the most important part of a presentation.*

Questions and Answers

Depending on the amount of time you have for your presentation, you may choose to have a question-and-answer period at the end. A question-and-answer period can contribute to your presentation by helping you clarify and expand points of special interest to the audience.   If your presentation is long, a brief exercise before questioning, or a 10-minute break that precedes questions gives you and your audience a chance to shift from presentation to interaction.

If you choose to take questions, here are a few recommendations.

- **Give guidelines**. Let your audience know when it is time for questions and specify how long that period will be.   For example, say, "We have about 15 minutes. Does anyone have comments or questions?"   If you don't set a time limit, you may find that your presentation drags on too long.

- **Repeat the question if you're addressing a large group.** This will ensure that everyone hears the question. For example, say, "Bob just asked me to clarify the deadlines for the sales program.   Let me go over those one more time."

- **Be concise and brief**.   Answer the question, but avoid over-answering.   If you spend five minutes answering the first question, you won't have as much time for others.

- **Don't argue with a questioner**.   This is not a debate.   If the individual persists, politely state points of agreement and move on. Your presentation should not become a forum for someone else's agenda.

- **Admit it if you don't know the answer to a question**.   Don't try to make up answers on the spur of the moment. Simply say, "I'm sorry I don't know the answer to that off the top of my head. Let me check on that for you."   Then make sure you do check and get back with the individual. You can defer to an audience member, but that takes time and shifts agenda.

- **End the meeting on time**.   Regardless of how lively or enjoyable the discussion, end the meeting on time. If you are able to stay, invite those who would like to continue the discussion to stick around.

Repeat the question if you're addressing a large group.

9

Ways to Close a Presentation

At the end of your presentation, you should lead your audience through an assessment of what it has learned one last time. This will not only help people to crystallize things in their minds, but will also help to clarify any confusion. You can do this in one of several ways:

- **Summary**. Conduct the summary or ask someone in the group to summarize the main points. Also reclarify any actions that need to be taken. For example, "We will have a newsletter designed and in the mail in two months. John, you will write the material and Ann, you will handle the production?"

- **Round-Robin**. Ask each member of the audience to say what he or she has learned or to commit to a task or action.

- **Ending with a laugh**. For example, ask everyone to stand, stretch for six seconds and then clap four times. Then bow and say, "Thank you for that standing ovation!"

- **Evaluation**. Either prepare a formal evaluation ahead of time or distribute index cards and ask audience members to write down what they thought of the presentation. Encourage them to do this before they leave and have them place their evaluations on a table by the door. If you allow them to be turned in later, you probably won't receive many back.

Lead your audience through an assessment of what it has learned one last time.

9

Regardless of what you include in your close, frame the close carefully. A technique to consider is to have at least three, perhaps four, different parts within your close. For example:

Frame the close carefully.

First: Summarize the section or part of the presentation just completed.

Second: Review the entire presentation, noting what you did, and stressing the benefits. Show your audience members how the information can be applied to their unique situation.

Third: Recite a parable, anecdote, or short, humorous story to make a key point and provide a nice contrast to the review.

Fourth: Tell a story, analogy, or situation relevant to the participants that touches them emotionally and will anchor the presentation in memory.

Fifth: A funny or touching poem that is relevant to the presentation can be shared.

Close Worksheet

Before your next presentation, decide how you will bring it to a close and note that below.

I will close my next presentation by

- Summarizing the following points: _____
  _____
  _____
  _____

- Listing these key benefits to my audience: _____
  _____
  _____
  _____

- Telling the following story, parable or poem: _____
  _____
  _____
  _____

- Listing these action steps: _____
  _____
  _____
  _____

- Evaluating the presentation.

    1. Evaluation form I will use: _____

    2. I distribute and collect the evaluation form.

9

Evaluations

Evaluations can prove to be a challenge for the presenter.

Evaluations can prove to be a challenge for the presenter. The key questions are when to introduce evaluations and how to handle them so as not to lose momentum from the presentation. Evaluations are the best way of achieving crucial feedback and can't be ignored.

After delivering an insightful, closing comment, pause and allow the audience to applaud. Acknowledge the response, then step forward and quietly request that they share their valuable insight with you via the evaluation.

Simplified Evaluation Form

Directions: On a scale of 1 to 5, with 1 being poor and 5 being excellent, rate the presentation on the following points:

1.   The presenter was credible. 1 2 3 4 5

2.   The presenter was articulate. 1 2 3 4 5

3.   The material was informative. 1 2 3 4 5

4.   The visuals added to the presentation. 1 2 3 4 5

5.   The room was comfortable. 1 2 3 4 5
(If you rated this 3 or below, tell why the room was uncomfortable.)

6.   The refreshments were good and well-stocked. 1 2 3 4 5

The main thing I learned from this presentation was: _____
_____

I would ☐   would not ☐ recommend this presentation to a friend.

Other comments: _____
_____

The single-most important factor when evaluating your presentation is whether your audience "caught" what you "threw at them." A customized evaluation form that lists your expectations is helpful for you, but when you make presentations on a regular basis, a more standardized form must be used to ensure consistency.

Of utmost importance, the form must be clear and require little work on the participant's part. They've done their work during your presentation!

> *The form must be clear and require little work on the participant's part.*

After Your Presentation

What you do after your presentation is just as important as what you did before. Following are some suggestions to help you tie up all those loose ends.

- **Network**. Immediately after your presentation, talk one-on-one with as many people from the audience as you can. Ask them what they learned and if there was anything else they wish you had covered. This information will be helpful to you if you're asked to give another similar presentation.
  Do not delude yourself: The people who most liked you and your presentation are most likely to be around after your talk. The people who were dissatisfied are usually long gone. There's great satisfaction in heavy, well-earned praise after your presentation. Bask in this time and enjoy it. Then realistically assess the truth.

If any associates saw your presentation, ask them for their evaluations. Consider the following when asking for critiques.

- Ask people whose judgment you regard highly and who will freely offer candid criticism.
- Request criticism on all aspects of the presentation: appropriateness of the topic, comprehensiveness of the material, clarity of organization and delivery and quality of the visuals.
- Accept all comments in a receptive and gracious manner.
- Evaluate the criticism honestly and objectively.
- Note comments so that you can incorporate corrective action into future presentations.

9

Critiquing your presentation will help you prepare for future ones. In addition to personally critiquing your presentation, ask others for their opinions. Their input will help you when you plan your next presentation.

Clearly note your gains: credibility and visibility.

- **Thank support personnel**. If a secretary or someone else in the office helped you coordinate your presentation, thank that person for helping. If the meeting was held away from the office, such as at a hotel, be sure to send the facility manager a thank-you note. If there were any problems, note them so they can be corrected in the future.

- **Clearly note your gains: credibility and visibility.** Review what you have gained through your presentation. Identify the credibility you acquired by making your presentation. Think about how you can capitalize on it more fully. Realize with whom you have gained visibility. What can you do to further it?

- **Evaluate yourself**.   Take a few minutes to evaluate your performance. Record your feelings about the setting, participants, comments and any other information of interest. Be sure to include any resources that you used and sketches of the seating arrangement, noting what you liked and disliked about it. Also, review techniques that did and did not work. This evaluation will help you in planning future presentations.

- **File your presentation materials**. Don't throw anything away, even if you don't think you will ever make this presentation again. First, you might be surprised by a request. Second, even if you don't give this exact presentation again, you may be able to use some of the overhead transparencies or research materials.

- **Keep your practice videotape**. Don't record over the videotape of your practice presentation. After you've made two or three more presentations, go back and review the original one. You'll be pleasantly surprised at how much you have improved.

- **Reward yourself for a job well done**. Treat yourself to a token reward. Weather permitting, take a brief walk outside or treat yourself to lunch at your favorite restaurant. Enjoy a performance, read a book, relax. A well-done presentation is emotionally and physically draining. Allow time to recharge.

9

Self-Criticism Checklist

Before I accept a speaking assignment ...

☐ Am I the right person for this occasion?

    • How will I be perceived by the audience? _____

    • My credibility to speak comes from: _____

☐ Do I have a message to send to this audience?

    • My main point is: _____

    • The thing I want my audience to do is: _____

☐ Can I make the time commitment to do the job right?

    • Preparation time needed: _____

    • Time allotted to present materials: _____

Once I've accepted the speaking assignment ...

☐ Do I have a plan for delivery?

    • Style

    • Content

    • Interaction

☐ Am I adequately prepared?

    • Properly organized?

    • Am I emotionally and mentally ready?

    • Are all materials ready?

☐ What kind of response do I anticipate?

☐ How can I assure that I am heard?

☐ Will my presentation be accepted in the spirit it is intended?

After I finish my presentation ...

☐ Did I accomplish my purpose?

☐ Do I have valid feedback about my presentation?

☐ How far did I divert from my plan?

☐ What could I have done better?

☐ What worked well?

☐ Do I need to do anything as a follow-up?

9

Questions for Personal Development

1. What is the major emphasis of this chapter?

    _____
    _____
    _____
    _____

2. What are the most important things you learned from this chapter?

    _____
    _____
    _____
    _____

3. How can you apply what you learned to your current job?

    _____
    _____
    _____
    _____

4. How will you go about making these improvements?

    _____
    _____
    _____
    _____

5. How can you monitor improvement?

    _____
    _____
    _____
    _____

6. Summarize the changes you expect to see in yourself one year from now.

    _____
    _____
    _____

Summary

- Bringing your presentation to a successful close is just as important as your opening.
- If you have the time for a question-and-answer period, let your audience know how much time you will devote to it. Then, end your presentation on time.
- Bring your presentation to a close by giving your audience an opportunity to think about what it has learned one more time.
- After your presentation, evaluate yourself and ask your audience and any peers who might have been present to do the same. Incorporate any corrective action into future presentations.

> *End your presentation on time.*

9

9

CHAPTER 10

The Manager's Role as Trainer

The final section of this book focuses on training skills for managers and supervisors. As a manager or supervisor, your primary function is to make sure that things get done. Training is at the heart of getting things done. You cause things to happen, ensure that they happen, and guarantee that they will continue to happen.

> *Training is at the heart of getting things done.*

Jim Siress, an international trainer and speaker, reminds managers of the risk in forgetting the responsibility of training. He tells of the many wonderful innovations of the Egyptians thousands of years ago.

- If one were to enter a pyramid today, one would still encounter an air cooling system so sophisticated that while the desert air may rise past 114 degrees, the air inside stays cool and refreshing. Engineers have yet to be able to replicate such a system.

- Reliefs on the walls of passageways are painted with a blue dye that has not faded over the ages. Designers have yet to be able to replicate a blue dye that retains its color as the Egyptian dye did.

- In the interior of the pyramid, there are mummies which are remarkably intact. Morticians have yet to replicate such a method for preserving the human body over thousands of years.

Although the ancient Egyptians were brilliant inventors, builders and engineers, they were poor managers. They never taught their

163

skills, never passed on their knowledge, and their society as they knew it ceased to exist. Businesses must find better ways to get things done. Employees must be taught and mentored throughout the organization. The way to get things done is through your staff. Even if your company has an in-house training department, with specific people designated to perform the training functions required, training is still part of your role and responsibilities. Departmental needs require you to include training and guidance, development and coaching with your associates.

It begins on the associate's first day in your department as you explain the activities of the company, the department, and the associate's responsibility with regard to those activities. It may include showing the associate how to do specific tasks. It could be a simple one-on-one meeting with a staffer to explain how to use the new fax machine or how to correct performance on a piece of equipment. It could be a scheduled day of instruction on a procedure or a change in the company. Impromptu and spontaneous, or planned and necessary, formal or informal — training is what allows the manager to pass on the knowledge and information that allows associates to function at an optimal level of performance. Training supports, facilitates and ensures growth.

Much of what you have learned in this book can be used in your training sessions. After all, a training session is nothing but a presentation of how to do something. The essentials remain the same: people, principles, preparation, practice.

In this section you will discover how to use what you have already learned about presentations to conduct effective training sessions for your associates. Additionally, you will learn the secret to motivating adults to learn and how to develop an effective training plan.

The way to get things done is through your staff.

Your Biggest Asset — Your People

A business's assets are not only the facilities, equipment, computers, machines, or assorted gadgets spread across a business place. The real assets are your people. By focusing on people and the enormous amounts of energy, innovation, creativity, caring and skills they bring to a job, businesses can more confidently enter the turbulent times of change and chaos.

But what do you do when your associates aren't successful, or your organization is not growing? This happens when there is a gap between how associates do their jobs and what you need them to do. Whenever you find such a gap, you have a training opportunity — a chance to make your associates winners.

The following ASSET Staff Training Model illustrates how you can use training to close the gaps. Let's analyze each part carefully.

The Japanese assess every aspect of a situation before they plan their strategy.

"ASSET" STAFF TRAINING MODEL

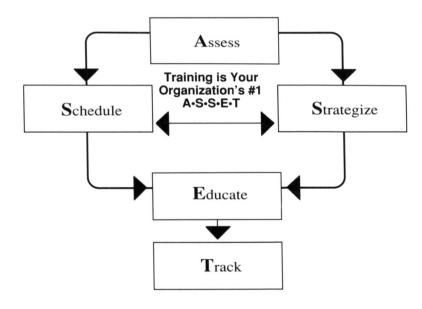

Assess

Training is Your Organization's #1 A·S·S·E·T

Schedule   **S**trategize

Educate

Track

10

Assess

The Japanese believe that one cause for the productivity gaps between them and Western society is that the Americans have "a fast trigger and slow bullet," while the Japanese have "a slow trigger and fast bullet." They assess every aspect of a situation BEFORE they plan their strategy and execution.

Regular assessment of your associates is important for several reasons.

*Assessment
ensures that what
must be taught is
taught.*

1. **It minimizes the risk that your training will take on a shotgun approach, without any specific direction.** Assessment of your employees' needs ensures that you will be proactive in your training instead of reactive. To be effective, training must be conducted for a specific reason: a reason that's exposed through effective assessment of your employee's performance. The *Koran* long ago counseled that "if you don't know where you are going ... any road will get you there." Without specific training objectives, anything *might* occur, but probably not what you would *like* to occur.

2. **Assessment ensures that what must be taught is taught.** Remember, training is used to close the gap between what your company expects and how your associates actually perform. If you train without first assessing what needs to be learned, you end up telling your associates what is *"nice to know,"* not what they really need to know.

3. **Assessment determines the *"must know."*** It specifies exactly what must be done and how it must be done to meet the company's mission in the most effective and efficient manner possible.

Time management experts all stress that excellent performance combines both efficiency and effectiveness. While efficiency means getting things done right, effectiveness means doing the right things. Employee development requires that the two not be mutually exclusive. Your associates improve through deliberate, planned training. The assessment tools on the following pages will assist you in determining the current "gaps" in employee performance.

Associate Performance Assessment

Name _____

Basic Responsibilities	Obvious Strengths	Obvious Weaknesses	Overall Assessment of Performance Historically (Superior, Average, Substandard)	Performance During Last Year

ON-THE-JOB TRAINING ASSESSMENT WORKSHEET

Team Member Name _____ Date _____

	Not Evident								Very Evident

On-the-job confidence: 1 2 3 4 5 6 7 8 9

Tolerance for stress: 1 2 3 4 5 6 7 8 9

Standards of excellence: 1 2 3 4 5 6 7 8 9

Attention to detail: 1 2 3 4 5 6 7 8 9

Innovation: 1 2 3 4 5 6 7 8 9

Flexibility/openness to alternatives: 1 2 3 4 5 6 7 8 9

Ability to teach, model: 1 2 3 4 5 6 7 8 9

Acceptance by peers/superiors: 1 2 3 4 5 6 7 8 9

Speed: 1 2 3 4 5 6 7 8 9

Commitment to job/organization: 1 2 3 4 5 6 7 8 9

People tolerance: 1 2 3 4 5 6 7 8 9

Self-starter: 1 2 3 4 5 6 7 8 9

Desire to excel: 1 2 3 4 5 6 7 8 9

Willingness to learn: 1 2 3 4 5 6 7 8 9

Responsive to constructive criticism: 1 2 3 4 5 6 7 8 9

Openness to new job direction: 1 2 3 4 5 6 7 8 9

Self-confidence/esteem: 1 2 3 4 5 6 7 8 9

Total _____

Schedule and Strategize

After the training need has been determined through assessment, it's time to schedule and strategize. It doesn't matter which you do first. Sometimes it may be more advantageous to schedule the training and then develop the strategy. This is often the case when the training is crisis-driven or when calendars are scheduled so heavily that people won't have time for training unless a time is cleared well in advance. At other times, it may be more advantageous to develop your training strategies to address short- or long-term organizational needs and then schedule the training.

When strategizing, you establish the "when," "how" and "who" of training. In doing this, there are some fundamental questions you should ask yourself.

When is the best time to hold a training session?

- **What are my most critical current problems and needs?** Identify the problems or needs you intend to address.

- **When is the best time to hold a training session?** Can you convene your team during a lunch break or should you have members come in early or stay late?

- **What are the demands my team faces?** If you are in the middle of the holiday rush, it may not be the best time to schedule a training session. It may be more advantageous to wait until after the first of the year.

- **How can my training be accomplished in the fastest and least costly manner?** If asking your employees to come in early or stay late necessitates paying them overtime, you may decide to hold two or three staggered training sessions so that your training can take place during the work day.

10

Additional questions critical to a strategy include:

Do you need classroom training, or would on-the-job discussions serve the purpose? Is a team meeting necessary or can a memo take care of the problem? Is a class outside the company more efficient than conducting the session in-house? Would it be more effective for the associate to attend a public seminar or should teams within the company attend training?

Wall charts can be useful in planning a training opportunity or establishing a strategy and schedule for a training endeavor. Charts give you a road map, generate additional questions, and pinpoint factors that need to be considered in order to arrive at the desired result. They are very useful to those not on the development team who need to be informed.

The questions and planning required in order to develop the most advantageous training plan grow out of the assessment. The ASSET Staff Training Model is a continuous process, with each piece building upon and referring to another.

Educate

Is a team meeting necessary or can a memo take care of the problem?

Managers must ensure that their associates can do the job and that their performance can help the company accomplish its objectives.

Twenty-five years ago companies hired people to perform set tasks and didn't ask them to do a lot of thinking. Twenty-five years ago most workers and even some managers learned their jobs by observation, experience and trial and error. But the rules have changed since then, and they continue to change. Workers today must understand their jobs and their equipment. As a manager, it is your job to educate your associates and make sure they know how to do their jobs.

There is a difference between education and training as well as between training and development. They need to be understood and respected by the managers and supervisors in order for all responsibilities to be met and for the associate to perform at an optimal level. Education disseminates knowledge and awareness and focuses on "what" information must be known.

Training provides task and skill capabilities. It teaches how tasks get done. Training focuses on improvement today while development stresses the investment for tomorrow. Each are necessary and each must be addressed differently in the process of attaining quality performance.

Track

Most often, performance gaps are identified when performance is tracked.

Tracking performance is important in helping you to determine the effects of your training. It also pinpoints any changes or improvements that need to be made. When tracking performance, you may even discover some additional training needs. If so, refer to the assessment portion of the ASSET Staff Training Model on page 165.

In your training programs you need to establish a way to track performance up front. For example, if your training is on the company's dress code, you can track your success by observing whether or not employees abide by the dress code. If your presentation is on increasing sales, you can track performance through sales figures.

Performance gaps are identified when performance is tracked.

10

ASSET Model Worksheet

Using the ASSET Staff Training Model, determine how you will close the gap between what your organization expects and what your associate delivers.

(Employee Name)   (Date)

Assessment (Describe the need.)

_____

_____

Schedule (When is the best time to hold this training?)

_____

Strategize

I will direct this training at (whom?) _____

_____

I will conduct this training by (how?) _____

_____

Educate

I will educate my associates on (subjects) _____

_____

Track

I will track the effectiveness of my training by (how?) _____

_____

10

Testing Your Knowledge Balance

Take a moment to complete this test and then check your answers, using the answer sheet on the following page.

1. Circle the names of real, not fictional people:

Jack Armstrong	Steven Jobs	J. Paul Getty
Slim Pickens	J.R. Ewing	Harry Houdini
El Greco	Ed Norton	The Elephant Man
Annie Oakley	Lizzie Borden	Lady Macbeth
Sergeant York	Ichabod Crane	Corporal Max Klinger

2. How about geography? Circle the real places:

Timbuktu	Xanadu	Camelot
Bali	Boys Town	Peyton Place
Atlantis	Yemen	Transylvania
Katmandu	Sri Lanka	El Dorado

3. Circle the items below that you can eat or drink:

Plaice	Ouzo	Pfennig
Farthing	Gherkin	Shoat
Rondelet	Ort	Dry Sack
Haiku	Caftan	Flan
Homily	Linguisa	Bombe

4. Fads come and go. Circle the decade for each fad:

Miniskirt	'20s	'30s	'40s	'50s	'60s	'70s
The Jitterbug	'20s	'30s	'40s	'50s	'60s	'70s
Swing Bands	'20s	'30s	'40s	'50s	'60s	'70s
Okies	'20s	'30s	'40s	'50s	'60s	'70s
Flappers	'20s	'30s	'40s	'50s	'60s	'70s
Bobby Soxers	'20s	'30s	'40s	'50s	'60s	'70s

5. Are the following people male or female?

E.B. White	Male	Female
Babe Didrikson	Male	Female
Alice Cooper	Male	Female
Osceola	Male	Female
Sandy Koufax	Male	Female
Jean LaFitte	Male	Female
Corazon Aquino	Male	Female
Hecuba	Male	Female
Benazir Bhutto	Male	Female

> *"Genius is 1% inspiration and 99% perspiration."*
> *Thomas Edison*

10

173

ANSWERS

QUESTION #1

- **Jack Armstrong** — Fictional radio character in 1933 program, "Jack Armstrong the All-American Boy."
- **Steven Jobs** — Real (1955-); person responsible for the development of Apple Computers.
- **J. Paul Getty** — Real (1892-1976); was one of the richest men in the world.
- **Slim Pickens** — Real (1919-1983); rodeo clown, television cowboy and movie actor.
- **J.R. Ewing** — Fictional television character on "Dallas."
- **Harry Houdini** — Real (1874-1926); Ehrich Weiss, considered a great escape artist and magician.
- **El Greco** — Real (1541-1614); Domencios Theotocopoulos, Spanish painter.
- **Ed Norton** — Fictional television character in 1950s program, "The Honeymooners."
- **The Elephant Man** — Real; John Merrick (1863-1890).
- **Annie Oakley** — Real (1860-1926); Phoebe Oakley was an expert sharp-shooter and rodeo performer.
- **Lizzie Borden** — Real (1860-1927); accused of murdering her father and stepmother with an ax.
- **Lady Macbeth** — Fictional character in the play *Macbeth* by William Shakespeare.
- **Sergeant York** — Real (1887-1964); Alvin York, United States hero in World War I.
- **Ichabod Crane** — Fictional character in *The Legend of Sleepy Hollow* by Washington Irving.
- **Corporal Max Klinger** — Fictional television character on "M*A*S*H."

QUESTION #2

- **Timbuktu** — Real town in central Mali.
- **Bali** — Real Indonesian island.
- **Atlantis** — Imagined island of Greek legend that sank into the ocean. Some think it may have existed.
- **Xanadu** — Imagined location in Samuel Coleridge poem "Kubla Khan."
- **Boys Town** — Real town near Omaha, Neb., founded by Father Edward Joseph Flanagan in 1917 for homeless boys.
- **Yemen** — Real Arabian country located on the Red Sea.
- **Sri Lanka** — Official name for the island of Ceylon, located southeast of India.
- **Camelot** — Imagined English Kingdom from *"King Arthur and the Knights of the Round Table."*
- **Peyton Place** — Fictional location identified in the 1956 book by the same title.
- **Transylvania** — Real region in Romania.
- **El Dorado** — Imagined place rich with gold in Spanish legend.

QUESTION #3

- **Plaice** — An American or European flatfish.
- **Farthing** — A former unit of British currency.
- **Rondelet** — A form of French poetry.
- **Haiku** — A form of Japanese poetry.
- **Homily** — A sermon.
- **Ouzo** — An anise-flavored Greek drink.
- **Gherkin** — A small cucumber used to make pickles.
- **Ort** — An uneaten morsel of food.
- **Caftan** — A long-sleeved, full-length garment.
- **Linguisa** — A spicy sausage.
- **Pfennig** — A unit of German currency.
- **Shoat** — A young hog.
- **Dry Sack** — A dry sherry.
- **Flan** — A custard tart.
- **Bombe** — A round, molded dessert.

QUESTION #4

Miniskirt:	'60s
Jitterbug:	'40s
Swing Bands:	'30s
Okies:	'30s
Flappers:	'20s
Bobby Soxers:	'40s

QUESTION #5

- **E.B. White** — Male, (1899-1985); American writer.
- **Babe Didrikson** — Female, (1914-1956); U.S. golfer.
- **Alice Cooper** — Male, (1945-); American rock singer.
- **Osceola** — Male, (1804-1838); Seminole Indian leader.
- **Sandy Koufax** — Male, (1935-); Baseball player.
- **Jean LaFitte** — Male, (1780-1826); French pirate.
- **Corazon Aquino** — Female, (1933-); former President of the Philippines.
- **Hecuba** — Female, mythological queen of Troy.
- **Benazir Bhutto** — Female, (1953-); former Prime Minister of Pakistan.

10

Finding the Answers

It's not important for you or your associates to know all the answers. But it is important that you know *how* to find them. As a leader, you have to be able to keep information flowing. You need to be able to help your team members find the right answers and then make them feel good about sharing those answers with others.

By recognizing the training role required of all managers, you can qualify your teams to do the job.

How did you do on the previous test? Did you answer all of the questions correctly? Probably not. And it probably is not necessary.

If we were to measure job performance based on the results of this test, what would this say about you, about your performance, about your effectiveness?

This illustrates an important point: the discrepancy between what is nice and fun to know vs. what is needed to know: *"must know"* vs. *"nice to know."* Many of the questions on the test probably did not relate to your business. They definitely provide important information for specific people and for specific jobs — but, they might not be things you need to know in order to perform your job at an optimal level.

For the manager and supervisor, this distinction is critical as you assess gaps and strategize solutions. A shrinking workforce with increased demands for quality and service make it essential that managers avoid "nice to know" training sessions and instead ask, "What do they need to know in order to perform their jobs well?"

> *It's not important for you to know all the answers; it is important that you know how to find them.*

10

Seeing Yourself as a Trainer

How do you see your job? Take a few minutes now and list your current job responsibilities and the approximate percentage of time you spend on each. For example, meetings may consume 10 percent of your time; training may consume 30 percent; and researching and writing reports may consume the remaining 60 percent.

_____ Meetings with employees
_____ Other meetings
_____ Training employees
_____ Completing reports
_____ Administrative tasks
_____ Other

How much time do you currently spend with your people?

How much time do you currently spend with your people? Hopefully, it's the majority of your time.

A recent time-efficiency study at a major chemical company in Iowa showed that more than half of the managers' work time was spent on managing people. When questioned, the managers said they felt that the time they spent with their employees was wasted or unproductive time because they weren't "doing" things. Here is a group of managers obviously unfamiliar with the work of Peter Drucker. They haven't grasped the concept that people are a company's major asset.

It is important for you to understand that your job as a manager or supervisor is *not* to "do" things, but to make sure things get done. The only way you can make sure that things get done is to spend time with your associates, equipping and training them to do their jobs well.

Training vs. Learning

Before you can begin training, it is important to think about how people learn. Remember your own formal schooling. In school you were given an assignment to read a book or memorize dates. Then you were tested to see how much you learned.

But did these tests really measure knowledge? Or did they simply measure the amount of information you were able to memorize and then retrieve? You learned how to get by, how to act and to do just enough to get the grade you felt was acceptable.

When you were tested, you probably received letter grades, such as an A, B or C or percentage grades, such as 100 percent, 90 percent or 80 percent. If you were like most people, it didn't take long to determine what kind of student you wanted to be. Maybe you were satisfied with being a "B" student. In that case, you did enough to achieve a "B."

Most of your team has been taught in this same way. As a result, you undoubtedly have associates who know exactly how many sick days they can take, just how far they can push you during a meeting and how long they can wait to do a project.

Before you can begin training, it's important to think about how people learn.

Your Challenge

Your greatest challenge as a trainer is to change the mindset of your associates from doing just enough to get by to doing their best all the time.

Nobody wants a "C" mechanic working on her car or a "C" doctor removing her appendix. Nor should you be satisfied with having a "C" associate on your team.

Don't waste time berating the system. It's time to make sure that everyone on your team is an "A" associate, not a "C" associate. We don't know if our doctor graduated at the top or bottom half of her peers. Lawyers aren't paid or ranked by their grade point. Professionals are paid based on their ability to "master" their discipline. The new thinking required by manager and associate alike is training and then performing to a specified level of mastery.

10

Questions for Personal Development

1. What is the major emphasis of this chapter?

_____

_____

_____

_____

2. What are the most important things you learned from this chapter?

_____

_____

_____

_____

3. How can you apply what you learned to your current job?

_____

_____

_____

_____

4. How will you go about making these improvements?

_____

_____

_____

_____

5. How can you monitor improvement?

_____

_____

_____

_____

6. Summarize the changes you expect to see in yourself one year from now.

_____

_____

_____

Summary

As a manager or supervisor, your associates are your biggest asset. If they do their jobs efficiently and effectively, you will have accomplished your number one goal, getting things done.

Before starting a training session, remember the acronym **ASSET** and use it to help plan your training. Follow the five steps:

1. **A**ssess your associates' training needs.

2. **S**trategize your training session.

3. **S**chedule your training session.

4. **E**ducate your associates.

5. **T**rack your associates' performances following training.

As a leader in the '90s, you don't have to know all the answers, but you do need to be able to find them when you need them. Similarly, you need to be able to help your associates find the answers they need to be winners.

In order to help your associates, it's important that you spend the majority of your time working with them — not shuffling papers. If you currently spend more of your time "doing" things rather than making sure things get done, you need to find a way to shift gears.

Before you can begin training, you need to understand how most of your associates have been taught in the past. Most, if not all of them, have been taught to do just enough to get by. Your challenge is to change this mindset. Your team shouldn't concentrate on doing just enough to get by, but on doing its best every day.

> *To help your associates, spend the majority of your time working with them — not shuffling papers.*

10

10

C HAPTER 11

Motivating and Training Adults

Before you can help an adult learn, you need to know what is really important to that individual — what motivates him to excel and want to become a winner on your team. Everybody wants to be a winner, to be part of a winning team. The question is, "How do you facilitate that need in a productive way?"

For example, is Betty interested in becoming an executive secretary or is she satisfied being a clerk-typist? If Betty's goal is to eventually become an executive secretary, it is your job to help her gain the skills she needs to advance. If, on the other hand, she is satisfied being a clerk-typist, you need to help her be the best clerk-typist she can be.

Train with the kind of impact that maintains their respect.

Training with Impact

How do you motivate adults to learn? The first thing you need to do is train with the kind of impact that maintains their respect — training in such a way that they don't turn you off. You don't want your associates to say, "Oh no, Jim's been to another training session. Now what is he going to want us to do differently?" or "Here comes Ann with her notebook. She'll badger us for a week and then things will go back to normal."

Taking Employees From What They Don't Know
to What They Know

Simply stated, your job as a trainer is to take your associates from what they don't know to what they do know. Let's examine this more closely. Look at the training model in the following diagram. This model illustrates how to move your employees from what they don't know to what they do know.

Study the model carefully because it can be confusing. When you think about what you know, there are things that you know you know and things that you don't know you know. Similarly, when you think about what you don't know, there are things that you know you don't know and things that you don't know you don't know.

Your job is to take your associates from what they don't know to what they do know.

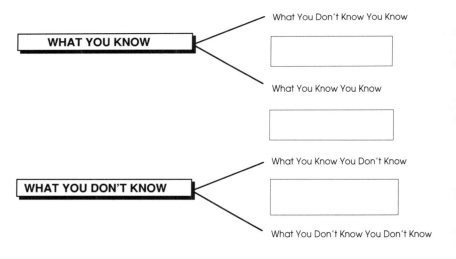

Let's look at an example of each using Bob, a new salesperson working for a computer retailer.

Case Study

What You Know

- *What You Know You Know:* Bob knows that he will sell XYZ-brand computers. He feels comfortable with that because XYZ is the same brand of computers he sold for his previous employer. Having sold XYZ computers before, Bob knows how they operate and what benefits to emphasize to customers. He knows the pricing structure and he knows the type of buyer that prefers his product.

- *What You Don't Know You Know:* In talking with his new boss, Bob learns that the company's invoicing system is the same as the one he used at his last employer. Thus, Bob has discovered something that he didn't know he knew. He also discovers that one of the on-line techs he worked well with was recruited to the company.

What You Don't Know

- *What You Know You Don't Know:* Bob is nervous because he knows that there are some things about his new job that he doesn't know. For example, this company has a service department, and Bob has been told that he will be responsible for selling service contracts, too — something he didn't do well at his last job. This is an example of something Bob knows that he doesn't know. Bob is also unclear about the unique financing arrangements of his new employer.

- *What You Don't Know You Don't Know.* What Bob is totally unaware of — or what he doesn't know he doesn't know — is that his new company will expect him to stay one-half hour to one hour after closing every night to complete his own paperwork. At his other job, a secretary completed all the final paperwork for the salespeople.

C
A
S
E

S
T
U
D
Y

11

The Trainer's Questions

If you were Bob's boss, it would be your responsibility to make sure that Bob knows everything he needs to know to successfully sell computers for your company. In doing this, you will need to explain to him both things he knows and things he doesn't know. This will entail training in the safe zone, the danger zone and the "aha" zone. Following is an explanation of each of these zones and tips on how best to train in each of them.

Most of your training should take place in the safe zone.

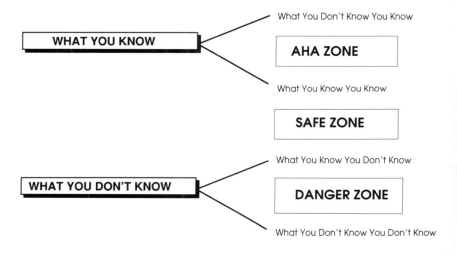

The Safe Zone

The path of least resistance occurs when working with associates on *what they know they know* and *what they know they don't know*. This is called the safe zone. This is where most of your training should take place.

Adults, and kids for that matter, learn best in a stress-free environment. When you train or make presentations that appeal to the safe zone, you set the learner's mind at ease and reduce the fear of failure.

In the example using Bob, what Bob knows is how to sell XYZ computers. What Bob knows he doesn't know is how to sell service contracts.

To successfully train in the safe zone, take the following steps:

- ***Review activities that a worker is comfortable with.*** For example, say, "Bob, I know you've sold XYZ computers before, but let's review the benefits together."

- ***Build a positive knowledge foundation.*** Ask open-ended questions that allow the learner to talk and explain what he knows. Your primary responsibility as a trainer is to build confidence.

- ***Push beyond the obvious.*** No one feels very positive by stating or discussing the very obvious. False praise or undue attention to the obvious will actually diminish your respect. Probe below the obvious by asking questions that uncover the learner's thinking, motivation and logic. For example: "Bob, you're right about the XYZ being a time saver for our customer, but what makes it such a good value?"

> ***Push beyond the obvious.***

The Danger Zone

When you tell your associates what *they know they don't know* and *what they don't know they don't know*, you are training in the danger zone. You are leaving familiar ground and treading on the unfamiliar. In Bob's case, what he doesn't know he doesn't know is that he will be expected to stay one-half to one hour after closing to do his own paperwork. If you don't position this information correctly or you place too much emphasis on the paperwork aspect of the job, he may feel discouraged and overwhelmed, and thus lose interest.

Training in the danger zone should be positioned carefully before you ever communicate it to your associates. It's best to surround danger-zone information with material from the safe zone. When you begin to tell associates about things *they don't know they don't know*, you risk having them become discouraged, or resistant. Many people simply do not want to change anything.

Without meaning to, managers often throw new associates into the danger zone during new-hire orientations. What often happens is that new employees are brought in for orientation, wide-eyed and excited. Then, for the next three hours they are bombarded with

11

everything they wanted to know, everything they didn't want to know and everything they didn't even think they needed to know. When that happens, somewhere along the line they go into overload and turn off.

Make the new seem familiar and the familiar seem new.

Usually, the first few days on the job is a honeymoon period when everything is new and exciting. But if you overwhelm new associates, you'll work twice as hard getting them to perform adequately. The most impactive time for employees is the first four hours on a new job. The first two days determine the rules — both written and unwritten — for what they must do and what they can get away with. Effective training is imperative.

A good rule for sharing information that your employees don't know is to **make the new seem familiar and the familiar seem new**. By making the new seem familiar, you take out the threat. For example, with Bob, say, "The paperwork we need you to complete includes all the basic information you get at the time of the sale, so it shouldn't take too long."

Similarly, by making the familiar seem new, you won't risk having people turn you off because they think they know what you are going to say. For example, say, "Let me show you how to take the information you gather at the time of the sale and put it into our sales reports."

To successfully expose danger-zone information, here are some things to remember:

- *Position unknown information around previous successes or skills.* Say to Bob, "I know that you were an effective salesperson in your company, and you certainly know the benefits of these computers. At our company, we are very proactive in our sales approach. Let me show you what I mean. Here we take every benefit and plan a sales presentation around it."

- *Clarify exactly what the desired performance will be.* For example, "During the first year, we expect you to sell $50,000 worth of equipment per month. I will monitor your figures closely and if you're having a problem reaching quota, we will address it immediately." Be specific or surprises will hurt your training efforts later.

- *Listen and watch for negative responses.* This includes shaking head, stuttering, disbelief or complete rejection of an idea. As a trainer, it's easy to get wrapped up in our content, failing to ensure that anyone's learning. Danger-zone information is critical to performance enhancement, but unrecognized resistance may result in miscommunication. You think they learned and they think you heard their "no."

- *Pay attention to your timing.* Danger-zone information is best accepted once a learner is comfortable with the content and the trainer, but not too tired. Do not enter the danger zone at the end of a long presentation.

- *Know the ratios.* Your training should only enter the danger zone a few times. A good rule is six to one — six safe-zone concepts to every danger-zone. If you must cover a great deal of "unknown" material, break it into smaller doses. Once resistance rises, learning stops!

The Aha Zone

Telling your associates what *they don't know they know* and *what they know they know* is considered training in the aha zone. You need to be cautious when training in this zone because people are often skeptical. They may say to themselves, "What's he trying to sell me? I knew that all the time," or "What's he trying to do, put me in my place?" Likewise, they could wander off mentally, marveling at this new information, and be totally unreceptive to further information.

For example, in the case of Bob, when you initially start talking to him about the benefits of XYZ computers, he will feel very comfortable. But if you get too basic or try to tell him too much information that he already knows, he may turn you off and begin to think, "I know that. Why is he telling me things I already know? I wish we'd get on with it."

Here are some key points when entering the aha zone:

- *Count the ahas.* Whenever persons see or hear something that rings true with their experience, they want to explore

> *Listen and watch for negative responses.*

the new finding. In short, they stop listening and start "playing" with their newfound information. Too many ahas and they'll hear little you say. A ratio of four to one is about right — four safe-zone ideas for every one planned aha.

- *Play the clock.* It's most effective in training to enter the aha zone before a break, or at the end of a presentation. That way they "play" on their time rather than yours!

- *Back up your ahas.* You must know what your audience knows so you can approach the aha zone effectively. Planned ahas are powerful behavior modifiers, but only if you can support the new information with facts. Be prepared for questions and have your facts prepared for every planned aha. A well-documented aha will stick with your learner. An unsubstantiated aha leads to resistance and lost opportunity.

Training with Impact

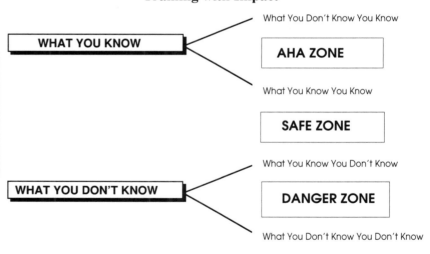

1. Training failure is reduced when we direct ourselves to the safe zone.
   - What do they know?
   - Why are they here?

2. Training in the danger zone should be positioned carefully before communicating it to another.
   - What do I have that will make a real difference?
   - Do I have any true "gifts" for them?

3. Training that is received cautiously is usually in the *aha zone*.
   - What information do I have that will cause a light bulb to go off?
   - Where have I gone that they have never been?

High Impact Training Worksheet

Professional trainers know that a secret to their success is founded on their impact factors. Using the space below, identify your impact factors:

The "Aha" Zone ...

-
-
-
-

The "Safe" Zone ...

-
-
-
-

The "Danger" Zone ...

-
-
-
-

11

What's in It for Me?

Small children are famous for asking "why?" Adults may get tired of answering that question, but in reality, adults want to know the same thing. Adults constantly want to know, "What's in it for me?" or "Why do I need to do that?" That's not a selfish way of thinking, it's very normal. How satisfied would you be if you were simply told to come in and do your job? Chances are, you wouldn't be very satisfied.

Everyone has his own motivations. Before you can successfully train your associates, you need to determine what motivates each one of them to learn. What's in it for them — your associates? Test everything you say and show with "So What?"

Adults will learn only what they feel a need to learn.

The Big Picture

Adults need to understand "the big picture" in order to see the relevance of your information and where they fit into the overall scheme of things. They will learn only what they feel a need to learn. It's important for the people you train to know what impact their actions will have on the big picture. For example, Mary will respond more positively to you if you say, "Mary, could you please complete this order request today? If you do, we can receive our materials by the end of the week and start on the new job." She won't respond as positively if you simply say, "Mary, get that order sheet completed today."

In the first example, Mary sees the importance of completing the order sheet, and she understands how completing the project on time depends on her doing her job. This motivates her to respond.

Training Adult Learners

Once you know how to structure your presentation for maximum adult learning, you need to know the most effective way to teach adult learners. People learn from what they hear, what they see and what they do. Approximately 70 percent of an audience is visually programmed. That is to say, people learn best by watching what is happening. Twenty to 25 percent of an audience is auditory, which means people learn best by hearing the spoken word, and only 5 to 10 percent of an audience is kinesthetic, meaning learning best through touch, feel and sensory perception.

With each preferred mode, memory is directly affected. Memory and increased ability to use what is taught are enhanced by teaching to the learner's preferred mode.

If you are training a group, your best bet is to combine all three methods. Tell your associates what they need to do, show them how to do it and then give them the opportunity to do it themselves. If you are working with an associate on a one-on-one basis, use the method he prefers. For example, if you are trying to teach associates to use a computer, you may have some people who will learn best by reading the instructions, others who will learn best if you tell them how to operate it and a third group of people who will learn best if you just let them sit down and figure it out for themselves, with you available for questions.

Twenty to 25 percent of an audience is auditory.

Training with the Preferred Modes

Visual learners prefer to have their training built around reading or viewing assignments. The visual learner's slogan could well be, "Seeing is believing." They rely on their ability to absorb information, taking in everything they see. The visual learner prefers printed directions, and is usually successful with policy manuals and checklists. The visual learner will look for documentation and support for what he learns. A visual learner would rather read a book than listen to a tape. Given a chance to watch a video, he would probably prefer it, although the follow-up work with a video must be written. Visual learners take in a lot of information but may not be able to do anything with it unless a written or very structured action plan is shown to them.

The MTV generation has become accustomed to color, motion, animation and high-impact graphics. Well-produced materials enhance every person's learning, but visual learners bring an interesting dimension to your training. They'll work with visual material (because they know and prefer looking at materials to

11

learn), but the trainer must build a concrete plan that can be followed.

You'll recognize visual learners when you talk to them. They are likely to use phrases like: "I see."; "Please show me ..."; "Can I read the documentation?" The visual learner will learn best when you translate his training into printed lists, with graphics and charts as support materials.

The auditory learner has a heightened preference for lecture, cassette tapes and materials presented with music. The auditory learner functions very well in discussion groups and is very comfortable following directions they've been given.

The auditory learner may miss information that is recorded poorly. How something sounds often dominates the learning, and it's common for the auditory learner to notice "how" something is presented more than "what" is presented.

Capturing travel time with cassette tapes is a preferred learning methodology for the auditory learner. As a manager, you may find your training efforts more effective if you watch an employee and record your observations on a tape as you watch. Note both positives and negatives and then make suggestions for corrective action. The auditory learner can play and re-play the tape, ensuring he "heard" it right.

You'll recognize the auditory learner by these comments: "I hear you."; "This sounds like a good deal." You'll also notice the auditory learner focusing on music, tones, rhythm and audience.

The kinesthetic learner prefers hands-on training. Lectures, videos, tapes and seminars all boil down to "doing" something for the kinesthetic learner. It's the manager's job to design training that is concrete, specific and do-able. One of the preferred learning programs for the kinesthetic learner is on-the-job training.

Repetition and measurable results are imperative for the kinesthetic learner. It's likely that the hands-on preference will cause the kinesthetic learner to ignore printed materials, and his desire to "do" something may cause his attention span to wander during a lecture or seminar.

You'll recognize the kinesthetic learner by these phrases: "How do I do this?"; "I feel ..."; and "Just step back and let me try." Trial and error is effective for the kinesthetic learner, but the manager must have patience with the errors and allow enough trials to create learning.

> *Visual learners use phrases like: "I see."*

11

Learning Preferences Worksheet

Watch your associates and identify how each member of your group prefers to learn.

Associate's Name	**Preferred Method of Learning**
_____	_____
_____	_____
_____	_____
_____	_____
_____	_____
_____	_____
_____	_____
_____	_____

Now identify ways you can incorporate all three methods into your training.

Visual:_____

_____

_____

Auditory: _____

_____

_____

Kinesthetic: _____

_____

_____

11

Training Turn-Offs

1. Lack of opportunity to practice

2. Lack of job relevance, meaningfulness

3. Training that doesn't focus on job concerns

4. Training that is academic or knowledge-based

5. Passive sessions

6. Long lectures, sitting too long

7. Uncomfortable surroundings (physical and psychological)

8. Not knowing where sessions are heading

9. Lack of instructor flexibility

10. Being made to feel incompetent, dependent

11. Being told what to do (without understanding why)

12. Lack of opportunity to talk

13. Formal, instructor-dominated session

14. Being taught to do things they will not have the opportunity, resources or support to carry out when back on the job

15. Wasted time, effort and training

Long lectures are a training turn-off.

Case Study

The Personal Side of Training

Eve is eight years old and small for her age, but she can't catch a ball. When a boy tosses her the ball, she lunges at it with a lack of coordination. Out of 10 easy tosses, she drops eight. But Eve is excited by the two she does catch, because she wants to join the Little League baseball team, just like her 10-year-old brother.

Eve's dad looks on as she pursues her ambition. The boys are polite, but clearly impatient, so Dad takes his little girl to the other side of the house for some private practice.

Using a tennis ball, he teaches Eve to follow it with her eyes as he tosses it up in the air and lets it drop. He instructs her to yell "NOW" just before the ball hits the ground. When she has learned to do this, he explains how she must never watch her hands or feet, but only the ball; and if she never takes her eyes off the ball, she is almost sure to catch it. Now he tosses her the ball and she catches it. Next, he tosses it about six feet over her head, and she catches it. During the practice, every time Eve misses, they analyze if she had remembered to keep her eye on the ball. After 30 minutes, Eve can "basket" catch nearly out-of-sight throws.

Then dad stages a contest with Eve and the boys, and Eve catches all 10 sky-high tosses. One of the boys catches nine, but the rest range from four to eight catches. Naturally, Eve is declared the winner.

What did Dad do to appeal to Eve's visual preference?

_____

_____

What did Dad do to appeal to Eve's auditory preference?

_____

_____

What did Dad do to appeal to Eve's kinesthetic preference?

_____

_____

CASE STUDY

11

Changing Behavior

Change is always a challenge. Self-esteem is at stake. Whether one is an adult or a child, fear of the unknown is always present in change. When jobs expand, responsibilities shift and new training is required, so your associates must cope with "change." With the accelerated change that all associates are experiencing, the manager must let the associate know that he is aware of these concerns.

Change is difficult. We are creatures of habit and often those habits make it possible to get a lot done with little thought or energy. It's so easy to turn on the auto-pilot and coast through a job or project without thinking. Doing what we have always done allows us to reduce the stress that occurs in daily living. Training must address with empathy and respect these very basic human reactions. The following three steps can help ensure growth:

> *Change is always a challenge. Self-esteem is at stake.*

1. ***Let the learner observe***. You perform the task while the learner watches, or you select an expert who can perform the job well. Your job is to explain how to do it and then demonstrate, making sure the associate sees the expected performance. First, describe what the learner should see. Relate it to the big picture and share why it is important. As the learner observes, emphasize the individual aspects and show him how to measure success. What does it look like as it's done?

2. ***Let the learner participate***. Once the individual has seen how to do the job, let him do it while you or a skilled associate supervises. There is a big difference between knowing what should be done and actually doing it. In this phase, the learner gets hands-on experience and you have the opportunity to see that the job is being done correctly.

3. ***Let the learner conduct***. In this phase, you turn the job over to the learner. Your role here is to observe and praise. Feedback is the breakfast of champions, according to Austin and Peters in their *Excellence* series. Feedback ensures that the job will get done and that the results are on track. There's a fine line between abandoning the learner and looming over him. You'll be most successful in step

three if you've done a good job in step one. Notice the combination of visual, auditory and kinesthetic learning styles. Watch and listen carefully at steps one and two for clues that the learner is uncomfortable. Step three appeals to the kinesthetic learner, but may leave the visual learner fearful. Don't forget the auditory learner throughout the process. Notice what the machine, when running well, sounds like. Pay attention to the sounds of success. There are sounds when things are improperly aligned, when things jam or when things are moving too slow or too fast. You'll notice the sounds if you take the time!

On-the-Job Components

Let the person perform simple parts of the job.

1. Show the person how to perform the task.
2. Explain key steps of the task.
3. Let the person perform simple parts of the job.
4. Coach the person through the entire task.
5. Let the person perform the whole job and observe what could be improved with corrective feedback.
6. Allow the person to perform on his own, but be available by phone or designate a contact person for support.

11

Developmental Training Worksheet

TASK _____ TITLE _____ DATE BEGUN _____ DATE ENDED _____

STUDENT _____ COACH _____ DEPT. _____

1. OBSERVING THE TASK	COMPREHENSION AND COMPETENCE	ADDITIONAL DEVELOPMENTAL NEEDS	MANAGER'S REMARKS
	SAT. GOOD EXCEL.		

2. PARTICIPATING IN THE TASK	COMPREHENSION AND COMPETENCE	ADDITIONAL DEVELOPMENTAL NEEDS	MANAGER'S REMARKS
	SAT. GOOD EXCEL.		

3. CONDUCTING THE TASK	COMPREHENSION AND COMPETENCE	ADDITIONAL DEVELOPMENTAL NEEDS	MANAGER'S REMARKS
	SAT. GOOD EXCEL.		

Most Common Failures/Causes of Instructional Breakdown

On-the-job training, team briefings and employee training offer tremendous productivity enhancements, but they can also be demotivators if handled poorly or incompletely. When productivity demands exceed employee skill, quality slips and often managers rush employees through training just to have a body assigned to the job. Unfortunately, six or seven months later, inadequate training has caused sagging production, inconsistent quality and staff frustration. As concerned managers, we document the performance and wonder why things are so bad. The truth is, the teacher failed and the student suffers!

Take a moment to review the 16 most common failures in instruction:

1. Failure to give instruction from the learner's perspective
2. Failure to take into account various levels of understanding
3. Message phrased in unclear terms
4. Excess of information that obscures intent
5. Burying clear intent under allusions, veiled references
6. Omitting essential pieces
7. Unnecessary threatening or enforcement of compliance
8. Failure to explain the conditions under which situation occurs
9. Inappropriate channel of message delivery
10. Departure from accepted custom without warning or explanation
11. False claims, promises
12. Lack of attention to learner's behavior
13. Evoking parent/child rebellious response
14. Self-destructive instructions
15. Failure to correct or praise in a timely manner
16. Inadequate incentives

> *When the teacher fails, the student suffers!*

Tips to Increase Your Training Effectiveness

The more involved your associates are in their training, the more beneficial the training will be. To encourage your associates' involvement, try some of these suggestions:

- **Plan participation**. Plan training that involves all learners in activities. For example, if you are conducting training on customer service, have your associates pair up and do role-playing, with one playing the customer and the other the customer service representative. Have several scenarios prepared ahead of time.

  Another way to elicit group participation is to ask two of your associates to role-play a situation before the rest of the group. Then ask the group to comment on what the "customer service representative" is performing.

- **Tell a story**. People get involved in stories, especially if you ask them to imagine themselves in the situations you describe. Say, "Imagine you are just beginning this job. It's your first day here, and . . ." Each member of your team then becomes the lead character in your story. Remember that your story should illustrate a point that is pertinent to the training objective.

- **Encourage the group to share leadership**. Ask for volunteers to lead small group discussions. Ask a second person to record each group's thoughts and report them to the entire training team. You can also ask one person to be the leader during the observation phase, another during the participation step and a third during the conduct phase. This makes everyone responsible for the knowledge exchange.

- **Call on someone by name and invite that person to comment**. Plan this step by inserting a signal in your training notes to stop and ask Alice or Zack about this particular topic. Ask someone who has not yet commented

Encourage the group to share leadership.

11

to offer an opinion, or call on someone who you know is especially good in a particular area. For example, say, "Sam, I know you've had a great deal of success in selling this equipment. Will you share your secrets for success with the group?" It is best if you can let the individual know this ahead of time so he can prepare a few comments. Make it clear, however, that all you need is a few comments. You don't want this person to get the wrong idea and take over your training session.

- **Stop the training every 20 minutes and ask one or more people to summarize what has happened so far.** This helps everyone review the important points discussed. It also helps break the monotony of a long training session and keeps everyone on his toes. (Rule of 20 — Exercise or Summarize!)

- **Give options rather than advice.** "Have you ever thought of ...?" works better than, "I think you ought to... ."

> *Give options rather than advice.*

- **Ask members of small groups to stand along a wall or beside their chairs after they complete a task.** This allows members to move around and encourages them to finish a task quickly.

- **Build in reflection time.** Take a break. Play soft music in the background while participants record their thoughts. The music discourages talking and encourages thinking.

- **Recognize emotions and body language.** If Tony's head shakes, say, "Tony, you're shaking your head. Would you share what you're thinking with us?" If participants begin to squirm or seem restless, it's time to take a break. Remember, training is hard work.

- **Ask whether the group has any questions, concerns or suggestions as you go along.** Members will appreciate your desire for input, and they may have important points to make.

11

Seven "Rs" to Remember

Effective training is remembered. Anything a trainer can do to encourage memory and foster recall should be considered. There are seven keys that help ensure your audience applies what they learn.

Relax: Prepare your audience's minds for new information by providing a relaxed atmosphere with music, humor or exercise. Release the tension as much as possible before the session. Build bridges between what they know and what you're going to teach.

Repeat new information.

Reflect: Have your audience review the training objective before the meeting or as an opening exercise, reflecting on what has prompted the training.

Read: Illustrate the new material. Visuals are useful. You might also send out advance reading or study materials. Often managers are afraid to ask their participants to do too much, because they are so busy; but, respect and value for the quality of your training rise when they must "earn" their way into the class.

Recite: Repeat new information. Small group interaction works well. Create several scenarios where the new information can be rehearsed.

Record: Write or draw the new information. Identify, chart and track learning milestones and benchmarks.

Respond: Interpret and critique the new information as it relates to old information. Build associations between the new and the old to cement the memory. Analyze and apply unfamiliar concepts to familiar situations to remember them more easily. Ask the learner about motivations and deeper understanding, using open-ended questions.

Review: By repeating and reviewing something new, the brain stores it in long-term memory so that it can be retrieved next week. Do you remember cramming for a test in school, learning the information just long enough to finish the test? Without relying on repetition and review, few of us could pass any of our high school final exams now!

Participation Worksheet

Complete the following worksheet before your next training session. It will help you decide what steps you can take to encourage participation.

Topic of training: _____

I will ask my associates to role play the following situations:

_____

_____

To make my associates feel like they are a part of this training, I will tell them the following story:

_____

_____

Member(s) of my team who could add something to this training session is/are:

_____

_____

Other things I will plan to do to promote participation are:

_____

_____

Your associates will get more out of your training if you find ways to involve them. By using the techniques discussed, you will make them feel more committed and involved in the learning process.

11

Questions for Personal Development

1. What is the major emphasis of this chapter?

   _____
   _____
   _____
   _____

2. What are the most important things you learned from this chapter?

   _____
   _____
   _____
   _____

3. How can you apply what you learned to your current job?

   _____
   _____
   _____
   _____

4. How will you go about making these improvements?

   _____
   _____
   _____
   _____

5. How can you monitor improvement?

   _____
   _____
   _____
   _____

6. Summarize the changes you expect to see in yourself one year from now.

   _____
   _____
   _____
   _____

Summary

Before you can help adults learn, you need to know what motivates them. Get to know your associates and find out what's important to them.

In order to keep your associates interested in learning, you need to train them in such a way that they will remain open and receptive to you. You will find that you are most successful when you train your associates in the safe zone — telling them what they know they know and what they know they don't know.

To motivate your associates to learn, take the following steps:

- Tell them what's in it for them.

- Show your associates how they fit into the big picture.

- Make your associates feel important.

- Allow them to observe, participate and conduct any learned task to ensure success.

When training adults, remember that they learn by seeing, hearing and doing. If you are involved in one-on-one training, train your associates in the method that works best for them. If you are training a group, use all three methods.

To ensure that your associates get the most out of training, encourage their involvement. This makes them feel they have a vested interest in a successful training session. It also helps them better grasp what you are trying to teach.

> *Get to know your associates and find out what's important to them.*

11

11

C HAPTER 12

Effective Listening, Questioning and Feedback Techniques

As stated earlier, your job as a manager or supervisor is to get things done. Getting things done is impossible if you don't communicate well with your associates.

The keys to good communication are listening, questioning and providing feedback. If you do these three things effectively, you will be able to communicate what you want and need to your associates so that they can do their jobs. Knowing how to listen well, question effectively and provide meaningful feedback to your associates will help you not only during training sessions, but also in your everyday contact with them.

Extensive studies done by British Airways identified specific behaviors that correlated with successful management, team interactions, customer service and leadership. Those behaviors most associated with success were supportive behaviors and clarifying behaviors. Supportive behaviors included affirming another's comments, and clarifying behaviors were summarization, testing understanding, and questioning.

> *"Nature has given to men one tongue, but two ears, that we may hear from others twice as much as we speak."*
> *Epictetus*

How Well Do You Listen?

When most people think of good communication, they focus on their ability to clearly tell another person what they want them to know. But hearing what the other person is saying is just as important.

If you're like most people, you probably think that you listen well. You hear everything people tell you, right? But do you really listen? Do you really comprehend what they are saying or are you so busy trying to formulate your next response that you miss their point?

The following quiz will help you discover how effectively you listen. Try to answer each question honestly and objectively.

The Listening Quiz

Answer by checking the spaces under "usually," "sometimes" or "seldom" to each of the following questions. When you talk with another person, do you ...

	Usually	Sometimes	Seldom
1. Look directly at the individual?	☐	☐	☐
2. Watch the individual, while listening to her?	☐	☐	☐
3. Decide from the individual's appearance and delivery whether she has something important to say?	☐	☐	☐
4. Listen primarily for ideas and underlying feelings?	☐	☐	☐
5. Determine your own biases, if any, and try to allow for them?	☐	☐	☐
6. Keep your mind on what the speaker is saying?	☐	☐	☐
7. Interrupt immediately if you hear a statement you feel is wrong or that you don't understand?	☐	☐	☐

12

	Usually	Sometimes	Seldom
8. Ensure that you've considered the other person's point of view before answering?	☐	☐	☐
9. Try to have the last word?	☐	☐	☐
10. Make a conscious effort to evaluate the logic and credibility of what you hear?	☐	☐	☐

Scoring Yourself on the Listening Quiz

On questions 1, 2, 4, 5, 6, 8 and 10 give yourself:

10 points for each answer of USUALLY
5 points for each answer of SOMETIMES
0 points for each answer of SELDOM

On questions 3, 7 and 9 give yourself:

10 points for each answer of SELDOM
5 points for each answer of SOMETIMES
0 points for each answer of USUALLY

If your score is:
90+   You are a good listener.
75-89   Not bad, but you could improve.
74 or less   You definitely need to work on your listening skills.

12

The Importance of Listening Well

The physicist, Isaac Rabi, who won the Nobel prize for his atomic research in 1944, attributed his success to the way his mother would greet him when he came home from school each day. "Did you ask any good questions today, Isaac?" she would inquire. Rabi commented, "There are questions which illuminate and questions which destroy. I was taught to ask the first kind."

Many of us are rewarded with a litany of discouragement: "Wait 'til I'm finished; then, if you still have questions ..." or, "Shoot first, and ask questions later." Adults learn to ask questions to show off their own acumen rather than to acquire information.

Effective listening skills enable you to respond appropriately to others. If you listen carefully to what your associate says, you can respond in an informed way. For example, if Paul says, "I don't understand why I have to do this," you can explain why it is important. Tell him, "I need you to write this report because you are the only person in the department who has a full grasp of the project." This answers Paul's question. If, on the other hand, you reply, "Paul, we all have a lot of work to do, and this report has to be done," you are not answering Paul's question.

In addition to providing your associates with appropriate responses to their questions, here are some other reasons why it is important for you to listen well.

- **You want your associates to talk freely and frankly to you.** If they believe that you don't listen to them when they have something important to say, the lines of communication will break down.

- **You want to know what is important to them**. If you listen attentively, they will be more likely to share information with you. This will ultimately help you communicate better with them on all issues.

- **You want them to furnish you with as much information as they can**. As a manager or supervisor, you need to know what is going on at all times. If your associates feel that you truly listen, they will be more apt to keep you informed.

On the following page are some typical phrases your associates will use and the appropriate action you should take.

> *"Some people talk simply because they think sound is more manageable than silence."*
> *Margaret Halsey*

12

Typical Phrase	Response	Your Action
"I don't know how."	Tell me what you can't do.	Teach them.
"I don't understand."	Help me understand.	Provide information.
"I don't want to."	How is this an issue?	Persuade them or sell them on value of what you want them to do.
"I don't see the value."	Help me understand.	Show the benefits.
"I don't have the authority."	What is it you are concerned about?	Give them ownership.
"I can't afford to."	What can you afford?	Reduce the risk or share the responsibility.

Tips for Effective Listening

Standing or sitting erect will help you focus on the person to whom you are talking and help you focus on what she is saying.

In addition to listening to what people say, you must train yourself to listen to what they don't say. Listen for pauses and silences and watch their body language. For example, if a person begins to frown, you know that she is unhappy. A wrinkled forehead often means confusion. Following are some tips to help you listen more effectively:

- **Express genuine interest by showing that you understand what the individual is saying.** For example, nod your head in agreement to show that you understand or say, "I understand, go on."

- **Express empathy**. For example, say, "John, I know that you are upset. Tell me what I can do to help. I want to listen."

12

- **Restate the problem or point**. Repeat to the person what you think she means. "So what you are saying is that you don't understand why we are making these changes."

- **Know when to remain silent**. If the individual is upset and trying to get something off her mind, it might be best to remain silent. Once that person has stopped talking, you can restate what you understand the problem to be.

What Effective Listening Tells the Other Person

When other people feel you are truly listening to their concerns, they will feel more important and positive about your responses to them. When you listen effectively, you are telling them several things:

- I know this is important to you.

- I am interested in you as a person.

- Even though I may not agree with what you are saying, I respect your right to say it.

- I don't want to judge or evaluate, I just want to understand you better.

- I want you to feel free to discuss anything with me.

Those who invest the time and effort necessary to improve their listening skills experience an increase in their effectiveness on the job, as well as in the quality of their training.

How to Know When You Are Listening Poorly

You may not even be aware when you are not listening. Here are some red flags that will help you know when you are listening poorly. Be aware of them and monitor yourself. If you notice these signs, you can refocus your attention on what is being said.

- **You are so busy formulating your reply that your thinking gets in the way of your listening.** This is a common problem. When you know exactly how you are going to respond before the person has finished her thought, you can't be listening very well.

- **You find yourself distracted.** While the person is speaking, instead of listening to her you are thinking about your plans for the weekend, looking out the window or slipping off into a daydream.

- **You dismiss the individual who is speaking as unimportant.** This is deadly. If you don't respect the person's opinion, you won't be able to give her an adequate reply. And, after all, that's why you must listen effectively in the first place.

- **You reach your conclusion of what the speaker is saying before the speaker finishes.** You may know some things, but mind-reading causes the listener to make serious assumptions.

You may not even be aware when you are not listening.

How to Know When You Are Listening Well

Just as there are clues to tell you when you are listening poorly, there also are clues to tell you when you are listening effectively. Following are some guidelines to let you know when you are truly hearing what an individual is saying to you.

12

- **You are able to repeat what has just been said to you**. For example, "What you want to know is ...."

- **You connect the body language with the verbal message**. You notice a wrinkled brow, so you move in closer to let that person know you understand.

- **You ask for a moment to frame your response**. You might say, "Let me think about that for a moment."

- **Regardless of whether you agree or disagree with what the person says, you respect her**. You don't look down on the individual or feel disgruntled by her comments.

Exercise

Now go back to the Listening Quiz. If you scored an 89 or below, make a list of the things you do that cause you to be a mediocre or poor listener. Next to each, write down some suggestions to help you overcome your bad habits.

I Don't Listen Well Because: **To Correct This Bad Habit I Will:**

_____   _____

_____   _____

_____   _____

_____   _____

_____   _____

_____   _____

Questioning Techniques

Just as important as listening attentively is the ability to question effectively. Through good questioning, you can obtain the additional information you need to communicate. If you don't understand what someone is saying to you, don't be embarrassed. The only dumb question is the one that isn't asked.

Questions are powerful communication tools. After all, if you ask the right question in the right way, you will get the right answer. If you don't ask questions or you ask the wrong question, you lose. Defense attorneys never ask a question to which they don't know the answer.

Questions keep you on target. They assure that you are meeting the other person's needs and they help you clarify exactly what those needs are. Good questioning is a necessary skill — one that needs continual development and fine-tuning.

When questioning someone, there are basically seven types of questions you can ask. Following is a description and example of each:

The only dumb question is the one that isn't asked.

1. **Factual.** This type of question helps you get additional facts. For example, "Can you clarify that?" Factual questions prompt an answer to the 5 W's: "who," "what," "where," "when" and "why."

2. **Explanatory**. Explanatory questions help you find reasons and explanations. You also can use them to gain additional information. For example, "How would this help solve our problem?" The continuous improvement discipline of Kaizen teaches people to get to the root cause of a problem by asking "why" five times. This assures the questioner she's received an accurate explanation of the true answer.

3. **Justifying**. A justifying question can be used to challenge old ideas and develop new ones. It makes people support their beliefs. For example, "What evidence do you have?" "How can you justify these costs?"

12

215

4. **Leading**. A leading question is used to advance a suggestion of your own or those of others. For example, "Why do you think this would be a feasible solution?" "You seem to be leaning toward this course of action, am I right?" A leading question prompts a conclusion and moves a discussion toward closure.

5. **Hypothetical**. Use a hypothetical question to introduce another suggestion or to change the course of the discussion. For example, "What do you think would happen if we did it this way?"

6. **Alternative**. Use an alternative question to encourage a decision. For example, "Which do you think is better, A or B?" Using an alternative question is a basic sales tool. By asking a buyer to select between two options, both of which are acceptable, the salesperson ensures that one of the two options is selected. This type of question helps the individual take control of an event or problem by forcing one of two options.

7. **Coordinating**. The purpose of a coordinating question is to help a group reach consensus. For example, "Do we all agree with this new plan?" This type of question acts as a synthesis of information. It prompts a summary and wrap-up.

Some words of caution: Too many questions can make the employee feel like she is being grilled. An unanswered question that is followed by more questions indicates that you didn't require or desire an answer to the first question. You send a message that it was not important. Remember, if you don't want an answer, don't ask a question.

Use an alternative question to encourage a decision.

Exercise

Complete this exercise to help you improve your questioning skills. For each of the seven types of questions, write down a typical question you could ask your associates. Then next to each, give the type of response you would expect to get.

Question   **Expected Response**

(Example)

1. Factual

"Larry, if the third week in June is not a good time   I would expect Larry to give
for you to take your vacation, can you tell me   me the exact dates he would
when would be a good time?"   like to take his vacation.

1. Factual

    _____   _____
    _____   _____

2. Explanatory

    _____   _____
    _____   _____

3. Justifying

    _____   _____
    _____   _____

4. Leading

    _____   _____
    _____   _____

5. Hypothetical

    _____   _____
    _____   _____

6. Alternative

    _____   _____
    _____   _____

7. Coordinating

    _____   _____
    _____   _____

12

Feedback

Feedback ties questioning and listening skills together. It ensures that ambiguity is reduced. There is an inherent ambiguity in many performance evaluations and training plans. For example, when told to "be enthusiastic" it's hard to interpret what it means. To smile more? Or work harder? Sweat more or work longer? Such abstract words require feedback to breathe meaning and results into the communication.

Performance requires feedback, and training is based on feedback. Providing feedback illustrates that you have listened to what someone has said, that you have observed what she has done and you have an opinion or suggestion to modify the act. Effective trainers send a message of confidence and purpose with the feedback they provide. People who have a high need for achievement thrive on feedback.

Both positive and negative feedback are important. When you provide negative feedback, you provide your associates with information needed to meet future expectations. When you provide positive feedback, you recognize their efforts.

Comments like: "Thanks for the good work!" or "You really did a super job on that report. It sure makes the department look good!" help you gain the respect of your employees. You will find them much more receptive to what you have to say if you build a trail of quality feedback. But you can undermine your credibility if you provide false praise or are afraid to confront real problems. You do a great disservice to your training efforts if you do not honestly provide feedback.

When providing negative feedback, take care with how you phrase the "negative." The very young have trouble with negative concepts. When confronted with the statement, "Don't slam the door," the child hears "slam the door." This problem carries over into adulthood. People have trouble interpreting negative instructions. Telling what "should not be done" doesn't necessarily narrow the field enough to enable one to know what one "should do."

Research indicates that instruction is difficult when it involves negative advice. A study by the Federal Aviation Administration contrasted affirmative instructions during an in-flight emergency with corresponding negative instructions. It found that people recalled 20 percent more from affirmative instructions (e.g., "extinguish cigarettes" vs. "don't leave cigarettes lighted" or "remove shoes" vs. "don't jump with shoes on").

In expressing positive feedback, follow these guidelines:

- **Express and state approval correctly**. Don't just think to yourself, "Joe did a good job." Tell Joe he did a good job and explain why you feel that way. For example, say, "Joe, you did a great job handling that customer's complaint. When she came in, she was really angry. But after you talked to her and explained the situation she seemed more than satisfied. I am sure she will come back again, thanks to you."

- **Express approval and appreciation reasonably often and according to each individual's needs.** Some people need to be told quite often they are doing a good job, while others may feel that if you say "thanks" too often, you are not being sincere. Gauge your appreciation accordingly. Positive feedback is a tool that should be used deliberately and strategically during training.

- **When appropriate, tell others about the good job your associates do**. For example, you might say to your boss, "Thanks for the kind words about the budget. Most of the credit goes to Bob, who put together all the figures." When you assume responsibility for training an individual, you also assume responsibility for building her credibility and reputation. Training may start in the classroom, but it usually ends in the hallways!

- **Place a copy of your associates' training certificates in their personnel files.** If your associates participate in training, be sure to include a certificate of completion in their personnel records. If one was not provided, a brief one- or two-paragraph memo can be drafted. But don't just slip it in a folder. Make sure they see it and then forward it to personnel. Build a sense of pride and accomplishment around satisfactory completion of every training effort.

> *"It has been proved that the deepest yearning of the human heart is for recognition — for honor!"*
> *Margery Wilson*

12

- **Express your appreciation by relating it to goals and expectations.** For example, say, "Sue, I really appreciate the fact that you stayed late to type that report so I could turn it in by the deadline." Relate your feedback to the purposes of the department, division or organization. This increases the value of their performance and the expectations that were met.

When You Must Correct Inappropriate Behavior

Not everything your associates do will garner praise. Sometimes it's necessary to correct inappropriate behavior or poor job performance.

When you must reprimand or counsel your associates, follow these guidelines:

"Honest criticism is hard to take, particularly from a relative, a friend, an acquaintance, or a stranger."
Franklin P. Jones

- **Focus your discussion on problems, procedures and results — not the individual.** For example, say, "Mary, this report is not acceptable. I asked you for comparisons going back 10 years, and you have given me the figures for only the last two years." Don't say, "What's the matter with you? Don't you listen? I said I wanted the figures for the last 10 years!"

- **Make sure it is feasible for your associates to do something about the problem.** For example, if Mary doesn't have access to figures for the last 10 years, she can't give you what you need. Don't blame her for an incomplete report. The trainer's responsibility is to empower employees, making sure they can do what's expected.

- **Be prepared to show your associates a better way.** For example, say, "Come into my office, Mary, and let me show you an easy way to compile this information."

Feedback Effectiveness Worksheet

Use the Feedback Effectiveness Worksheet below to assess your current strengths and weaknesses regarding giving feedback.

1. Did I take the time to know all the facts?

2. Did I explain the specific behavior I wanted to change?

3. Were my questions closed-ended or open-ended?

4. Did I communicate the reasons the change was required?

5. Did I include myself in the problem?

6. How did I provide opportunities for change?

7. What minimum standards did I communicate?

8. Did I offer positive consequences for when change occurs?

12

Exercise

Given the guidelines for delivering positive and negative feedback, write what you would say or do in the following situations.

1.   Lynn has just closed the largest sale ever recorded in the company's history.

_____

_____

2.   You've received calls from two clients who have complained that Jerry has missed several appointments.

_____

_____

3.   Jim has earned an award in his particular area of expertise.

_____

_____

4.   Barbara went over budget on her last project.

_____

_____

5.   Sally was supposed to have her report on your desk this morning. It's not there and you have just learned that Bill didn't give her the information she needed to complete the report.

_____

_____

6.   You just received a complimentary letter from a customer about the way she was treated by Neil.

_____

_____

7.   Your boss tells you what a good job your department did on your last big project.

_____

_____

Exercise

Take a moment and list all the things your associates have done in the last month that you consider achievements. Then indicate whether or not you provided them with feedback and, if so, what.

Achievement	Feedback (Reward)
_____	_____
_____	_____
_____	_____
_____	_____
_____	_____
_____	_____

If you can't think of more than five instances, you're not providing your staff with enough feedback. You are definitely not providing enough opportunities for success. Find ways to increase the amount you give. Feedback, both positive and negative, is important to your associates. Be sure to provide them with feedback on a regular basis.

Recognition Worksheet

List below the names of your associates and the way each prefers to be recognized. Use this chart to help you with your recognition efforts.

Associate	Recognition Preference (public/private)
_____	_____
_____	_____
_____	_____
_____	_____
_____	_____
_____	_____

12

Your associates need feedback in order to do their jobs correctly. When they perform well, it is important that you let them know that they are doing a good job, using the type of feedback they most appreciate. When they fail, you must also let them know. When you do, be direct and specific so that they can change their behavior and enjoy future success.

?

Questions for Personal Development

1. What is the major emphasis of this chapter?

    _____
    _____
    _____
    _____

2. What are the most important things you learned from this chapter?

    _____
    _____
    _____
    _____

3. How can you apply what you learned to your current job?

    _____
    _____
    _____
    _____

4. How will you go about making these improvements?

    _____
    _____
    _____
    _____

5. How can you monitor improvement?

    _____
    _____
    _____
    _____

6. Summarize the changes you expect to see in yourself one year from now.

    _____
    _____
    _____
    _____

12

Summary

Whether you are making a presentation, conducting training or simply talking with your associates one-on-one, good communication is imperative. If you listen, question and provide feedback effectively, you will be an effective communicator and manager.

Asking the right questions assures that you meet your associates' needs by clarifying exactly what those needs are. It helps you express concern and lets your associates know their importance to you.

Effective listening is also a communication requisite. It enhances the benefit of asking the right questions and helps you comprehend the information you receive through questioning.

Everyone needs to receive performance feedback, whether it's positive or negative. Providing your associates with the appropriate feedback allows them to do their jobs better. Feedback guarantees growth.

Negative feedback must be given immediately after the performance. If it cannot be provided within 24 hours, it has minimal effectiveness and is often perceived as overly critical. It must be done each time any individual performs below expectations.

Expressing appreciation and approval correctly and at appropriate times will encourage your associates to learn. When you must criticize, be sure to criticize the problem, procedure or result and not the individual. Then, make sure she can do the job. Be ready to show her how it can be done more effectively.

> *"As I grow older, I pay less attention to what men say. I just watch what they do."*
> *Andrew Carnegie*

12

12

C *HAPTER 13*

Your Training Style

Now that you know how to motivate your associates to learn, it's time to get down to the job of training. You can use many of the presentation skills that you learned in the first two sections of this book during your training sessions. However, there are many other techniques you can use to make your training both interesting and effective.

> *The first step is to understand the different ways in which instruction is given.*

Identifying Your Training Style

First, while you may be very effective as a manager or supervisor, understanding the science of training provides you with a discipline that allows you to repeat your successes. The first step in understanding the science of training is to understand the different ways in which instruction is given.

Think about your most valuable learning experience as an adult. Write down what occurred with regard to the instructor or trainer. How were you taught? What did the instructor do? What tools were used? How long did it last? What did you like?

_____

_____

Review the characteristics that came to mind. In all probability they can be categorized into quantifiable terms and practices that can be packaged into a style that's reproducible. What you have done is to describe the way you learn best. Just as people have different learning preferences (verbal, auditory or kinesthetic), preferences also show up in training styles.

Generally, most people train using the same style in which they are most comfortable learning. Yet, to be a truly effective trainer, it is important for you to recognize and understand the various ways others prefer to learn. We learn best when instructed in that style. The University of Missouri at Kansas City found that test scores could be significantly elevated by matching teacher style to learner preference.

So how can we determine the best style for individuals and audiences? By assessing our own preferences.

The following test will help you determine your personal learning preference. After you have completed this test, you will find out about the various learning styles, and how to use them to your advantage.

> *"The reasonable thing is to learn from those who can teach."*
> *Sophocles*

The Learning-Model Instrument

Take a few minutes and answer the 20 questions listed on the next two pages. Don't spend a lot of time thinking about your answers; simply mark your initial responses. If you don't have a preference, mark the one you find to be least bothersome. When you're finished, transfer your answers to the scoring sheet on page 231.

The Learning-Model Instrument
by Kenneth L. Murrell

Instructions: For each statement, choose the response that is truer for you, circling either "a" or "b."

1. When meeting people, I prefer:
   a. to think and speculate about what they are like.
   b. to interact directly and ask them questions.

2. When presented with a problem, I prefer:
   a. to jump right in and work on a solution.
   b. to think through and evaluate possible ways to solve the problem.

3. I enjoy sports more when:
   a. I am watching a good game.
   b. I am actively participating.

4. Before taking a vacation, I prefer:
   a. to rush at the last minute and give little thought beforehand to what I will do while on vacation.
   b. to plan early and daydream about how I will spend my vacation.

5. When enrolled in courses, I prefer:
   a. to plan how to do my homework before actually attacking the assignment.
   b. to immediately become involved in doing the assignment.

6. When I receive information that requires action, I prefer:
   a. to take action immediately.
   b. to organize the information and determine what type of action would be most appropriate.

7. When presented with a number of alternatives for action, I prefer:
   a. to determine how the alternatives relate to one another and analyze the consequences of each.
   b. to select the one that looks best and implement it.

8. When I awake every morning, I prefer:
   a. to expect to accomplish some worthwhile work without considering what the individual task may entail.
   b. to plan a schedule for the tasks I expect to do that day.

9. After a full day's work, I prefer:
   a. to reflect on what I accomplished and think of how to make time the next day for unfinished tasks.
   b. to relax with some type of recreation and not think about my job.

13

10. After choosing the previous responses, I:
    a. prefer to continue and complete this instrument.
    b. am curious about how my responses will be interpreted and would prefer some feedback before continuing with the instrument.

11. When I learn something, I am usually:
    a. thinking about it.
    b. right in the middle of doing it.

12. I learn best when:
    a. I am dealing with real-world issues.
    b. concepts are clear and well-organized.

13. To retain something I have learned, I must:
    a. periodically review it in my mind.
    b. practice it or try to use the information.

14. In teaching others how to do something, I first:
    a. demonstrate the task.
    b. explain the task.

15. My favorite way to learn to do something is by:
    a. reading a book or set of instructions or by enrolling in a class.
    b. trying to do it and learning from my mistakes.

16. When I become emotionally involved with something, I usually:
    a. let my feelings take the lead and then decide what to do.
    b. control my feelings and try to analyze the situation.

17. If I were meeting with several experts on a subject, I would prefer:
    a. to ask each of them for his opinion.
    b. to interact with them and share our ideas and feelings.

18. When I am asked to relate information to a group of people, I prefer:
    a. not to have an outline, but to interact with them and become involved in an extemporaneous conversation.
    b. to prepare notes and know exactly what I am going to say.

19. Experience is:
    a. a guide for building theories.
    b. the best teacher.

20. People learn more easily when they are:
    a. doing work on the job.
    b. in a class being taught by an expert.

13

The Learning-Model Instrument Scoring Sheet

Instructions:

1. Transfer your responses by writing either "a" or "b" in the blank that corresponds to each item in the Learning-Model Instrument.
2. Now circle every "a" in Column 1 and in Column 4 and circle every "b" in Column 2 and in Column 3.
3. Next, total the circles in each of the four columns and write the totals on the lines at the bottom of each column.
4. Then add the totals of Columns 1 and 2 and plot this grand total on the vertical axis of the Learning Model for Managers on the next page and draw a horizontal line through the point.
5. Now add the totals of Columns 3 and 4. Plot that grand total on the horizontal axis of the model and draw a vertical line through the point.

The intersection of these two lines indicates the quadrant of your preferred learning style.

Abstract/Concrete		Cognitive/Affective	
Column 1	Column 2	Column 3	Column 4
1. _____	2. _____	11. _____	12. _____
3. _____	4. _____	13. _____	14. _____
5. _____	6. _____	15. _____	16. _____
7. _____	8. _____	17. _____	18. _____
9. _____	10. _____	19. _____	20. _____

Total Circles ___

Grand Totals

13

231

Reproduced with permission from *The University Associates Instrumentation Kit*, San Diego, CA; University Associates, Inc., 1988

Learning Model For Managers

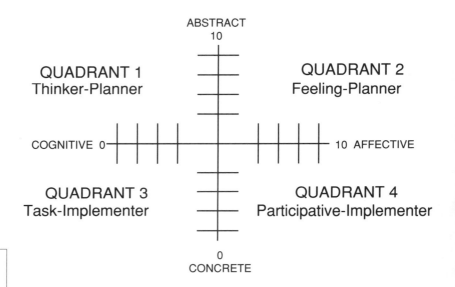

Learning is based on how we think and how we feel.

About the Learning-Model Instrument

The Learning-Model Instrument introduces four types of learning based on an individual's preference for cognitive or affective learning and concrete or abstract experiences. Stated simply, learning is based on how we think and how we feel.

In the model a scale ranges from 0 to 10 between cognitive and affective. This score measures your preferred style of learning new information . Although there are no pure choices or preferences, most people fall to one end of the spectrum or the other. You also plotted your score on the concrete-abstract scale, which indicates how you wish to experience training: "hands-on" or in theory/data presentation.

13

The horizontal axis represents the way people prefer to learn — using either a cognitive or an affective mode — because learning comes not only through thinking or cognition, but also from feelings and emotions.

The vertical axis represents the way people tend to experience training. If you prefer to experience training in a concrete way, then you prefer contact with real objects. You need to be able to physically touch and manipulate things in order to understand them. If you prefer the abstract, you like to deal with the world in thinking terms and by manipulating ideas or thoughts. You understand things best once you have them set in your mind.

How Understanding Your Style Helps You Train

> *"What is education but a process by which a person begins to learn how to learn?"*
> *Peter Ustinov*

As a manager or supervisor, you are likely to train in a style you are most comfortable with and in which you like to learn. Yet, in order to effectively train your associates, you need to recognize and respond to their diversity and variety in learning styles.

You will be most effective if you can adapt your style to the individual needs of your associates and/or the situation. Understanding each of these four learning quadrants will help you do that.

By understanding the four quadrants, you also will understand the relationship between your actions and the learning styles of your associates. To be effective, you must be capable of functioning well in all four quadrants, especially if you expect to face a variety of situations and challenges on the job.

Although you may prefer one type of training and preparation, you need to operate effectively in all of them. To be truly effective as a trainer, you need to flex your style among the different quadrants, depending upon what you are trying to accomplish and with whom you are working.

Now let's look more closely at each of the four learning quadrants.

13

Quadrant 1: The Thinker-Planner

An individual in Quadrant 1 has a combination of cognitive and abstract preferences. This "thinker-planner" is task-oriented. His environment usually contains things like numbers or printouts. Accountants and computer analysts generally fall into this category.

The thinker-planner treats things abstractly, often ignoring social and emotional elements during a presentation. These individuals tend to use models, theories or acronyms to catch attention and then describe what is to follow. The thinker-planner usually does well in training and education and has a talent for planning and organizing.

Strengths: logical, precise, systematic

Weaknesses: nit-picky, inflexible, boring, academic, bookish

The thinker-planner is task-oriented.

Quadrant 2: The Feeling-Planner

The individual who falls into Quadrant 2 has a combination of affective and abstract preferences. The "feeling-planner" is a thinker who enjoys working with people, but who doesn't want to get too close to them. Managers in this quadrant can often think through and understand the social and emotional factors affecting a large organization.

The feeling-planner uses stories, poems, jokes or humor to illustrate what he is trying to get across. If you fall into this quadrant, you probably will use lots of stories and examples to make your point in presentations.

Strengths: supportive, easy-going and emotionally-connected

Weaknesses: tendency to be conforming or permissive (Difficulties sometimes arise when good supervisors who are naturally people-oriented — feeling-planners — are promoted into positions that prevent them from having direct contact with others. They often feel like they are "out of touch" with their associates.)

Quadrant 3: The Task-Implementer

The Quadrant 3 individual has a preference for a combination of the cognitive and concrete. The "task-implementer" primarily wants to understand the task and focus on the details and specifics in a thoughtful manner. If these people are allowed to think about a situation, they can see the concrete issues and after close examination, make a well-thought-out decision.

The task-implementer is often a task-focused doer. If the interpersonal-skill demands are low and if the emotional work environment is not a problem, this person is likely to do well.

The task-implementer feels most comfortable training by giving his associates specific directions: "When this happens, you do this." These individuals like to use workbooks and to have structure in their training presentations. This is where the "how to's" and application power of training occur.

Strengths: determined, objective, concise, organized

Weaknesses: domineering, unfeeling

Quadrant 4: The Participative-Implementer

The participative-implementer has good people skills.

The individual in Quadrant 4 has a combination of affective and concrete preferences. The "participative-implementer" has good people skills and enjoys working closely with others. This is the quadrant where implementers and highly skilled organizational-development consultants usually reside. Public relations representatives and fund-raisers can often be found in Quadrant 4.

The participative-implementer likes to get involved. He has the ability and interest in working with the emotional needs and demands of people in an organization. The participative-implementer also enjoys experiential learning with lots of activity.

Strengths: enthusiastic, imaginative

Weaknesses: overbearing, unrealistic

13

Understanding Your Score

Scores indicate preference, not ability. It is unlikely to see any scores at either extreme on either axis. No single type is best. Any mixture of preferences simply represents a person's uniqueness.

The smaller the box drawn by the intersecting lines, the greater the flexibility to go beyond the boundaries of your preference and to "flex" into or use the other quadrants. The larger the box caused by the intersecting lines, the more locked in you are to those noted preferences, the more rigid you are, and the more difficult it is to train in the other styles. The actual preference is indicated by the long line of the box.

No one type of learning is best. If you scored five on each axis, you are likely to learn in multiple ways, to be extremely flexible and to have little problem training in all four quadrants.

Once you've identified your training need and understand your audience, it's time to develop your training plan.

> *"They know enough who know how to learn."*
> Henry Brooks Adams

13

Training Styles Worksheet

Name	Thinker-Planner	Feeling-Planner	Task-Implementer	Participative-Implementer	Remarks
1.					
2.					
3.					
4.					
5.					
6.					
7.					
8.					
9.					
10.					
11.					
12.					
13.					

Action Steps ...

1.

2.

3.

4.

13

Questions for Personal Development

1. What is the major emphasis of this chapter?

_____
_____
_____
_____

2. What are the most important things you learned from this chapter?

_____
_____
_____
_____

3. How can you apply what you learned to your current job?

_____
_____
_____
_____

4. How will you go about making these improvements?

_____
_____
_____
_____

5. How can you monitor improvement?

_____
_____
_____
_____

6. Summarize the changes you expect to see in yourself one year from now.

_____
_____
_____
_____

Summary

People tend to train in the same style in which they are most comfortable learning. In this chapter you learned about the various learning preferences and identified your own personal learning style. You also identified the learning preferences of your associates. This information will help you in future training sessions.

Regardless of what domain you scored the most points in, understanding how individuals in the other quadrants think and prefer to learn will help you in your training. When training, remember the following:

To be a truly effective trainer, you need to flex your style among the different quadrants.

- **Quadrant 1**. Thinker-planners are task-oriented. These people have a talent for planning and organizing. We are in this quadrant whenever we lecture, give an overview, demonstrate facts, figures and points.

- **Quadrant 2.** Feeling-planners enjoy working with people, but don't want to get too close to them. These people like to think things out completely before proceeding. We are here whenever we share stories, anecdotes, parables, a joke or poem to make a point.

- **Quadrant 3.** Task-implementers are task-focused doers. These people like structure and are methodical in their thinking. We are in this quadrant when we focus on "how to" applications.

- **Quadrant 4.** Participative-implementers enjoy working closely with others. They enjoy experiential learning with lots of activity. We train in this quadrant whenever we set up exercises, involvement or group activities.

13

> *"Creative minds have always been known to survive any kind of bad training."*
> Anna Freud

13

C HAPTER 14

The Art of Training

Once you've identified your training need and understand your audience, it's time to develop your training plan. Before taking this step, however, there are several important points to consider.

When to Train

The more formal the training, the less likely your people are to relax.

It may sound simple, but it's important to know when to hold training sessions. In determining when to train, you need to consider two issues:

1. **Whether to conduct a formal training session.** Does the problem you have identified require training or is there another way to resolve the issue? The more formal the training is, the less likely your people are to relax. Informal looks better, but you must prepare. Formal and informal are descriptions of style, not presenter preparation.

2. **The best time to train.** Once you've determined that you have a definite training opportunity, you need to decide when to hold your training session.

> *"Training is everything ... cauliflower is nothing but cabbage with a college education."*
> Mark Twain

Let's look first at determining whether training is truly necessary. A training opportunity exists whenever there is a gap between what your company expects and what your associates deliver. For example, let's say your company expects your department to sell $80,000 worth of equipment a month, but your staff is only selling $75,000. If this is the case, a training opportunity exists.

A training session is appropriate whenever you decide that the value of improved performance is greater than the cost of training. This gap should be written down and it should be one measure of whether your training was effective. In the example just cited, your department, in effect, is missing its sales goal by $60,000 a year. If you can conduct a training session that costs less than $60,000 and that will help your staff sell $80,000 worth of equipment or more per month, then you have a good training opportunity.

But do you need to hold a training session? Or is there a better way to handle the situation?

First, let's discuss identifying training opportunities. There are many signals that may indicate a training opportunity exists. Think about some of the signals in your company. The following checklist will help.

14

Trends Checklist: Training Opportunities

☐ Productivity is low or slipping.

☐ Customer service is not as good as it should be.

☐ Too much material is being wasted or there is a high incidence of damaged goods.

☐ Employee morale is low.

☐ Employees are taking too long to perform their jobs.

☐ Inaccuracy or shoddy workmanship is becoming a problem.

☐ The company's profits are stagnant.

☐ Deadlines are not being met.

☐ The company's market share is shrinking.

☐ There has been an increase in absenteeism and/or tardiness.

☐ The turnover rate of the work force is on the rise.

☐ Management is faced with labor disputes.

☐ There are increasing problems with recruiting qualified workers.

These are danger signs for your organization that should trigger action on your part. If any one of these is present, a training opportunity exists. Knowing these signs will help you analyze training opportunities in your organization. Be sure to repeat this exercise on a regular basis. Problems that don't exist now may crop up later.

The ability to identify these trends is an important skill in diagnosing when there are training issues to tackle.

14

Exercise

List the top three indicators or trends in your organization that tell you there is a performance problem. (Use the Trends Checklist to give you ideas or write your own.)

1. _____

2. _____

3. _____

Explain how each indicator or trend can be improved through training.

1. _____

2. _____

3. _____

Four-P Needs Assessment

Once you've determined that there is a training opportunity, you need to determine if a training session is the best answer or if there is another way to handle the situation. For example, can you meet one-on-one with a specific associate? Do you simply send out a memo? Or, is it best to meet with the group as a whole?

To help you determine whether to schedule a training session, use the following Four-P Needs Assessment. Ask yourself, will the training session evolve into a worthwhile use of space and time with regard to purpose, participants, property and plan? If any of the four Ps is missing, consider the alternatives: a memo, facsimile, phone call, coffee break or closed-door meeting with the key associates.

Ask yourself the following questions in each of the four categories. If you can't answer all of these questions, consider postponing or eliminating the training session until you have the answers and the resources.

Purpose

- What is the current training opportunity this session will address?
- What must I do in order to prepare for this training session?
- What information needs to be distributed?
- What do I want to accomplish in this training session?

Property

- What resources, facilities, materials, information or equipment are needed for this training session?

Participants

- Who needs to take part in this training session?
- Do I need any outside assistance in making my training presentation?

Plan

- Could this training be accomplished through any alternative communications?

      — memos, letters or reports, facsimiles
      — electronic mail, voice mail or telephone calls
      — teleconferences or satellite conferences
      — videotapes
      — individual conversations

> *"In life it is training rather than birth which counts."*
> *Ihara Saikaku*

14

The Best Time to Train

If all of the four Ps are present, you need to schedule a training session. In determining when to schedule the session, consider the following points:

- **Busy times**: Don't plan training sessions around busy times. For example, if Tuesdays are especially hectic for your team, don't schedule a training session on a Tuesday. Or, if Christmas is a busy season, steer away from planning any significant training commitment around that time of the year.

- **Holidays**: Avoid planning training too close to holidays. For example, don't schedule training for the day before a three-day weekend. If you do, you may find your associates distracted because they're thinking about their upcoming plans.

- **Vacations**: Before scheduling a training session, check your team's vacation schedule. If you plan training for a time when an associate is on vacation, she will either miss your message, resent being asked to change vacation plans or put the "monkey" on your back to get her up to speed with those who did attend.

Tips for Scheduling Training

Use the following guidelines when scheduling your training sessions.

- Check to find out when the room you need is available.

- Check the availability of audio/visual resources, especially if you need equipment for your training session, such as a videotape recorder/player and a television monitor.

- Avoid Monday mornings and Friday afternoons. This is when your associates will be thinking more about the weekend than what you are trying to tell them. Wednesday a.m. is the preferred training time in corporate America.

- Never plan a training session that includes more than seven hours of formal instruction. If you do, your associates will be mentally overwhelmed.

- Allow yourself enough time to prepare. Don't plan your session so soon that you can't fully prepare yourself.

The Training Flow Chart

Now that you have scheduled a training session for your associates, you need to concentrate on what kind of training they need. The following Training Flow Chart provides a visual of the complete process you should go through every time you decide to train your staff.

The flow chart is divided into three sections. The upper portion of the chart — Needs Assessment and Training Demand — notes the *why* of your training activity. The middle section — Strategy, Goal and Objective — is the *what*. And the bottom portion — Tactics and Outcome — concentrates on the *how*. Break out each section of the flow chart and examine it more carefully.

Allow yourself enough time to prepare.

14

The Training Flow Chart

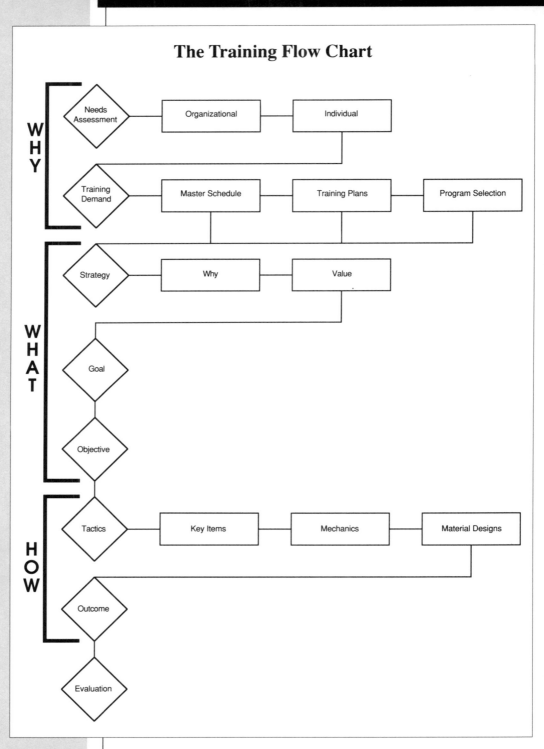

Needs Assessment

Whenever there is a gap between what the organization wants or expects and what an associate is doing to meet that expectation, you have a training opportunity. For example, let's say your associates have not been following the company's dress code, but the owner says she wants you to ensure that all employees follow it. Therefore, you need to find a way to get your associates to follow the dress code. In this example, and in most training instances, a needs assessment identifies three needs:

1. The need of the organization

2. The needs of the people who will be trained

3. Your needs — what it will take to make this training successful

Training Demand

Training is the process you use to close the gap between what the organization wants and what the employees need. Using this same example, your training demand is to make sure your employees understand the company's dress code and then follow it. It is at this point that you identify what must be done to close the gaps.

Strategy

Strategic training puts the manager in the driver's seat of the desired outcomes. A good strategy starts with what the outcome should be and then builds an approach to get there.

The strategy you use to convey management's concern about following the dress code is your instructional content. What do you say and how do you demonstrate it? In the dress code example, you might use the following strategy:

Strategic training puts the manager in the driver's seat of the desired outcomes.

14

1. Note specific instances of associates not following the dress code.

2. Call a short staff meeting to review the dress code with associates.

3. Give all associates a copy of the dress code.

4. Ask your team members if there is anything about the dress code they don't understand.

5. Ask if there are particular reasons why they are not following the dress code. For example, because some associates work in a drafty area they may be wearing sweaters over their uniforms, which is against the dress code.

What do you hope will happen as a result of your training?

Goal

In the goal statement, the trainer declares in writing what the outcome will be and how to measure the training's success. A goal is more than a target — it's a result of effective training.

What is your goal? What do you hope will happen as a result of your training? In the example we've given above, your goal will be to get all employees to abide by the dress code.

Objective

How will training help you achieve your goal? Generally, behavioral results are clearly defined in the training objectives. A good rule for your objective is to start every statement with the words: "As a result of this training, the participants will be able to ..." In this example, training will help ensure that all employees know about the dress code, that they understand what it means and that they have no problems abiding by it.

Tactics

A specific set of training steps will usually be listed as tactics. The three steps, observe, participate and conduct, are an example of a tactical training approach.

How will you conduct the training? If only one associate ignores the dress code, you may choose to meet with her individually and talk one-on-one. However, if several of your associates ignore the dress code, you may want to conduct a group meeting.

Outcome

Ask yourself what you want from your associates. What specifically do you want them to do as a result of this training? Using this same example, the outcome you desire is for all of your associates to follow the dress code.

Evaluation

Through the training evaluation process, you either will find that your associates have given you what you asked or that their performance is less than you desired. An evaluation measures the success of both the student and the teacher. Both should walk out of the training with expectations, knowing habits that should be changed and information that must be applied. In the dress code example, you determine if your training worked by observing your associates. If they all follow the dress code now, you know that your training was a success. If some are still not following the dress code, you need to go back to the top of the Training Flow Chart and start over.

An evaluation measures the success of both the student and the teacher.

14

Training Plan Worksheet

When a training opportunity is identified, use this worksheet to help you plan the best approach.

Needs Assessment:
The problem is _____
_____

Training Demand:
The training demand is _____
_____

Strategy:
To address the problem I will _____
_____

Goal:
By conducting this training, my goal is to _____
_____

Objective:
Achieving my goal will _____
_____

Tactics:
The tactics I will use to achieve my goal are _____
_____

Outcome:
The desired outcome I want is _____
_____

Evaluation:
After training was completed, I observed _____
_____

14

Developing a Training Plan

Whether your training is formal or informal, conducted during a one-hour team meeting or an entire week-long endeavor, the more carefully you plan the details, the more efficient and effective your training will be. The more you organize your thoughts and materials ahead of time, the more likely you will be to get the training results you want.

The Training Plan

When developing your training plan, there are five areas to work on. Copy the "Developing Your Training Plan" worksheet and use it every time you plan a training session. Note that these five areas correspond with sections of the Training Flow Chart on page 248.

1. Strategy

2. Goal

3. Objective

4. Tactics

5. Outcome

The more you organize ... ahead of time, the more likely you will be to get the training results you want.

14

Developing Your Training Plan

STRATEGY
Why is this training being conducted?

What does this training mean to your customers?

Internal customer:

External customer:

GOAL
What do you want to accomplish?

OBJECTIVE
What instructional expectations exist?

TACTICS
What are the three key items?
1.

2.

3.

What presentation materials will you use?

Date:

Time:

Room arrangements:

Number of participants:

Equipment:

OUTCOME
How will your audience respond?

1. To ...

2. To ...

3. To ...

14

Strategy

Why is the training being conducted?
1.   Why you are conducting this training session
2.   What the training means to your customers, both internal and external

Goal

What do you want to accomplish? It is important to know up front what you hope to accomplish. It is important to relay your goal to your associates at the beginning of the training session. This gives direction to your presentation and helps your participants understand what you expect. You should be able to summarize your goals in one statement of 25 words or less.

Summarize your goals in one statement of 25 words or less.

Objectives

What instructional expectations exist? What do you want to accomplish? In stating objectives for your training, follow these three simple guidelines:
1.   Be specific and concrete. State what needs to be done when, where and how.
2.   Be positive and optimistic. Expect success and avoid using negatives such as *not* and *never*.
3.   Be realistic and practical. Set an objective that is attainable and measurable.

Tactics

What are the three key items? Or what do you need to do to achieve your objectives?

Next, list the presentation materials you will need and the training session logistics. This information should include: date and time of the session, room arrangement, number of participants and equipment needed.

Outcomes

How will your audience respond? This is the final step in developing your training plan — identifying your outcomes. Each outcome on your list should be measurable.

14

Questions for Personal Development

1. What is the major emphasis of this chapter?

    _____
    _____
    _____
    _____

2. What are the most important things you learned from this chapter?

    _____
    _____
    _____
    _____

3. How can you apply what you learned to your current job?

    _____
    _____
    _____
    _____

4. How will you go about making these improvements?

    _____
    _____
    _____
    _____

5. How can you monitor improvement?

    _____
    _____
    _____
    _____

6. Summarize the changes you expect to see in yourself one year from now.

    _____
    _____
    _____
    _____

14

Summary

In determining when to train, you must first decide *if* training is necessary. If so, you need to consider the best time to train. When you schedule training is vital to the overall success of your mission.

The Training Flow Chart helps you determine what training is needed. It also helps you identify why you are conducting training, what you hope to accomplish through your training and how you will meet your training objectives.

The Training Plan helps you focus in on your strategies, goals, objectives, tactics and outcomes. Creating an outline gives you your content and framing your thoughts helps you bring your training together.

As a supervisor or manager you are faced with making presentations and training your associates on a regular basis. Knowing how to make powerful presentations and conduct effective training sessions will not only make you more confident in your job, but will make you invaluable to your company.

Knowing how to make powerful presentations ... will make you invaluable to your company.

14

Index

YOUR BACK-OF-THE-BOOK STORE

Because you already know the value of National Press Publications Desktop Handbooks and Business User's Manuals, here's a time-saving way to purchase more career-building resources from our convenient "book store."

ORDER FORM

- IT'S EASY ... Just make your selections, then mail, call or fax us your order. (See back for details.)
- INCREASE YOUR EFFECTIVENESS ... Books in these two series have sold more than a million copies and are known as reliable sources of instantly helpful information.
- THEY'RE CONVENIENT TO USE ... Each handbook is durable, concise and made of quality materials that will last you all the way to the boardroom.
- YOUR SATISFACTION IS 100% GUARANTEED. Forever.

60-MINUTE TRAINING SERIES™ HANDBOOKS

TITLE	YOUR PRICE*	QTY.	TOTAL
8 Steps for Highly Effective Negotiations #424	$14.95		
Assertiveness #4422	$14.95		
Balancing Career and Family #415	$14.95		
Change: Coping with Tomorrow Today #421	$14.95		
Customer Service: The Key ... Customers #488	$14.95		
Dynamic Communication Skills for Women #413	$14.95		
Empowering the Self-Directed Team #422	$14.95		
Fear & Anger: Control Your Emotions #4302	$14.95		
Getting Things Done #4112	$14.95		
How to Conduct Win-Win Perf. Appraisals #423	$14.95		
How to De-Junk Your Life #4306	$14.95		
How to Manage Conflict #495	$14.95		
How to Manage Your Boss #493	$14.95		
How to Supervise People #4102	$14.95		
Listen Up: Hear What's Really Being Said #4172	$14.95		
Managing Our Differences #412	$14.95		
Motivation and Goal-Setting #4962	$14.95		
A New Attitude #4432	$14.95		
PC Survival Guide #407	$14.95		
Parenting: Ward & June ... #486	$14.95		
Peak Performance #469	$14.95		
The Polished Professional #426	$14.95		
The Power of Innovative Thinking #428	$14.95		
Powerful Communication Skills #4132	$14.95		
Powerful Leadership Skills for Women #463	$14.95		
Powerful Presentation Skills #461	$14.95		
Real Men Don't Vacuum #416	$14.95		
Self-Esteem: The Power to Be Your Best #4642	$14.95		
SELF Profile #403	$14.95		
Shortcuts to Organized Files and Records #4307	$14.95		
The Stress Management Handbook #4842	$14.95		
Supreme Teams: How to Make Teams Work #4303	$14.95		
Techniques to Improve Your Writing Skills #460	$14.95		
The Write Stuff #414	$14.95		

MORE FROM OUR BACK-OF-THE-BOOK STORE

Business User's Manuals — Self-Study, Interactive Guide

TITLE	RETAIL PRICE	YOUR PRICE	QTY.	TOTAL
The Assertive Advantage #439	$26.95	$22.95		
Business Letters for Busy People #449	$26.95	$22.95		
Dealing with Conflict and Anger #5402	$26.95	$22.95		
Hand-Picked: Finding & Hiring ... #5405	$26.95	$22.95		
High-Impact Presentation and Training Skills #438	$26.95	$22.95		
Learn to Listen #446	$26.95	$22.95		
The Manager's Role as Coach #456	$26.95	$22.95		
The Memory System #452	$26.95	$22.95		
Parenting the Other Chicks Eggs #5404	$26.95	$22.95		
Taking AIM On Leadership #5401	$26.95	$22.95		
Prioritize, Organize: Art of Getting It Done #453	$26.95	$22.95		
Sex, Laws & Stereotypes #432	$26.95	$22.95		
Think Like a Manager #451	$26.95	$22.95		

SPECIAL OFFER:
Orders over $75 receive
FREE SHIPPING

Subtotal	$
Add 7% Sales Tax *(Or add appropriate state and local tax)*	$
Shipping and Handling *($3 one item; 50¢ each additional item)*	$
Total	$

VOLUME DISCOUNTS AVAILABLE — CALL 1-800-258-7248

Name_____ Title _____

Organization _____

Address _____

City _____ State/Province _____ ZIP/Postal Code_____

Payment choices:

❏ Enclosed is my check/money order payable to National Seminars.
❏ Please charge to: ❏ MasterCard   ❏ VISA   ❏ American Express

Signature X _____ Exp. Date_____ Card Number _____

❏ Purchase Order # _____

MAIL: Complete and mail order form
with payment to:
National Press Publications
P.O. Box 419107
Kansas City, MO 64141-6107

PHONE:
Call toll-free **1-800-258-7246**

FAX:
1-913-432-0824

Your VIP No.: 705-008438-098